CRACKERJACK POSITIONING

Niche Marketing Strategy For The Entrepreneur

Don Reynolds, Jr.

Atwood Publishing
Tulsa

Library of Congress Catalog Card Number: 92-74170
ISBN: 0-9634110-4-7

Cracker Jack® is a registered trademark of Borden, Inc. This book has been neither authorized nor endorsed by Borden, Inc.

Book Design: Susan Coman
Cover Design: Janet Drye
Cover Photograph: Bob McCormack
Typesetting: Protype, Inc.

Printed in the United States of America

For information on Mr. Reynolds speaking and consulting availability, audio-tapes, and/or newsletter, phone **1-800-662-4732**

Dedicated to
my delightful wife, Rose,
and to
Terry and Jean,
true friends in all seasons.

Contents

Chapter 1. Toy Surprise Inside

What makes Cracker Jack snack food different is the toy surprise inside the box. Crackerjack positioning is the process of discovering, accepting, developing and capitalizing on your toy surprise **1**

Chapter 2. Color Outside The Lines

Paradigm thinking limits creativity. It convinces you to color *inside* the lines. You've got to look outside the lines to find a viable niche. Exercises and examples teach you how to expand your thinking **9**

Chapter 3. Fill Your Medicine Pouch

A crackerjack position is developed by collecting information from a variety of sources and allowing a niche to evolve. Sculptor Harry Jackson illustrates how to use your medicine pouch in this process **19**

Chapter 4. Dance With The One Who Brung You

When you dance with the one who brung you, you focus on strengths instead of weaknesses. Individuals, athletic teams, businesses, and even cities are successful when they build on strengths **23**

Chapter 17. Either Price Or Value, Not Both

Today's market does not have room for enterprises attempting to be all things to all people. One decision you must make is to focus on either price or value. Peking Garden and Egg Roll Express demonstrate the difference

Chapter 18. No Trust, No Chance

Customers won't do business with you unless they believe you can satisfy their needs. This credibility is easier to achieve when you have a clearly communicated niche. People call Domino's for pizza delivery because they trust Domino's can satisfy their need

Chapter 19. Focus Your Resources

Your resources are limited. Focusing these resources on the single task of achieving and maintaining a niche is the key element to crackerjack positioning

Chapter 20. Name Supports Your Position

An important resource is the name of your enterprise. Ideally it should describe your niche. At the very least your name should be an asset and not detract from your strategy

Chapter 21. Be A Tortoise, Not A Hare

A simple strategy consistently followed will establish a crackerjack niche position. Diversions complicate and delay reaching your goal. Learn how Warner's strategy destroyed Knickerbocker Toys and why Bob Newhart has been on prime time television longer than any other performer

Chapter 22. Look For Red Cars

Driving through traffic you won't notice red cars until you narrow your focus and look for them. Today's business environment is constantly changing, providing opportunities to strengthen your position. You won't see the opportunities unless you look for them. See how the Nugget Casino and Touchstone Pictures first recognized then capitalized on opportunities

Chapter 23. Before Country Was Cool

The purchase of a bankrupt radio station in the country's poorest six-station market was followed by the successful development of a profitable niche in that market. This experience convinced the author that crackerjack positioning concepts work

Chapter 24. Nothing Replaces Commitment

If you are not willing to commit to implementing the strategy then all your other work will be in vain. See what others like Katherine Hepburn and Jack Nicklaus have accomplished through commitment. Learn what you can do to be equally successful

Chapter 25. Motivation Drives Commitment

People are motivated in a variety of ways. Motivation drives commitment. Learn what is the strongest motivational force and how you can incorporate that force into your strategy

Chapter 26. Listen To Carolyn Miley

Carolyn Miley didn't know anything about crackerjack positioning but following her advice is the key to making your strategy work

Acknowledgements

Some years ago Maureen Stapleton won a Motion Picture Academy Award for Best Supporting Actress. Her acceptance speech was short and to the point. She said, "I want to thank everybody I've ever known in my entire life."

And I want to do the same because everybody I've ever known has contributed to this book. Nonetheless, there are a few people without whose specific help this book would not have been written. My wife Rose, and Terry Johnson and Jean Kelley, to whom this book has been dedicated, were with me from inception to completion. It would not have happened without their love and support.

Juanell Teague helped me find the right track. Peggy Fielding taught me that writing a book is a messy process. Sally Dennison kept me from going off on too many tangents. Cork Milner reviewed my work and said, "Yes, you can write." Michael Larsen provided suggestions that added personality. Linda Boyd made sure the grammar and punctuation were accurate. Janet Drye created the magnificent cover. Jay Conrad Levinson wrote a spectacular introduction. Susan Coman held my hand as we designed the book. Richard Daniels and Michael LeBoeuf encouraged me to press on when I was discouraged. My children, Greg, Liz, and Don provided their love and support.

My father introduced me to the power of niche positioning. Don Roy helped me refine the concepts. My clients continue to teach me as much about crackerjack positioning as I teach them. Finally, I am grateful to the unselfish mentoring and overwhelming support I have received from the membership of two magnificient organizations: The National Speakers Association and Toastmasters International.

Foreword

I am pleased and privileged to introduce you to *CRACKERJACK POSITIONING* — both the concept and the book.

Author Don Reynolds has taken a topic and rearranged the principles so that you need not be a *Fortune 500* company to put them into practice. The genius in the book is that the principles are now custom-tailored *for the entrepreneur.*

Most entrepreneurs suffer from what the *Harvard Business Review* calls "resource poverty." Don Reynolds shows you how to rise above this poverty, how to make your small size an asset, and how to achieve your goals without the brute force of a gigantic marketing budget.

Best of all, the book shows you how to do these things with confidence and simplicity.

Rarely have I encountered a book that puts forth such valuable information in such a readable and engaging manner. *CRACKERJACK POSITIONING* is a lot of fun to read — even though it is extremely instructive. That means you'll look forward to reading it, and you'll learn for life the ideas it generously provides.

There's a warm, personal style that you'll find within the covers of this book. Sure, you'll find many secrets of successful positioning. And you'll read many case histories of people such as yourself.

When you've completed this book, you'll have more positioning insight that most of your competitors will ever have. Score one point for your team.

Although you'll probably return again and again to specific chapters of the book, the good Mr. Reynolds offers it to you in such a way that you'll remember most of it forever. And the results will glow on your bottom line.

Marketing is really a simple function — unless you are intimidated by it. Since most business owners are, they ignore marketing or make it too complicated. *CRACKERJACK POSITIONING* removes the mystique from marketing, shows how simple it can be, and gives owners of small business the confidence to market with verve and success.

When I wrote my first *Guerrilla Marketing* book, my motivation was to provide a book for the marketing-minded entrepreneur — since no such books existed. All the marketing books were written for companies with megabudgets. If I had read *CRACKERJACK POSITIONING*, perhaps I never would have written *Guerrilla Marketing*. Don Reynolds has accomplished exactly what I wanted to achieve — the realistic, non-textbooky approach to marketing that any business owner could embrace.

You are a lucky person in my opinion. You're lucky for five major reasons:

1. You're lucky to be on the brink of reading a very enjoyable book, a real page-turner all the way through.

2. You're lucky to be on the threshold of learning crucial truths about succeeding in small business.

3. You're lucky to be on the edge of losing any fear you may have of the marketing process. You're about to love it.

4. You're lucky to have discovered a book that reveals honest-to-goodness secrets of marketing success.

5. You're lucky to have been blessed with the guts to leave the corporate grind and go out on your own — to be your person as an entrepreneur.

When you combine the luck I've just mentioned with the solid information you're about to gain by reading *CRACKERJACK POSITIONING*, you'll have put a winning combination together. I congratulate you on your decision to call your own shots, and I commend you on the head start you are giving yourself by reading and absorbing this fine book.

Jay Conrad Levinson
Author of *Guerrilla Marketing*
Marin County, California

"Toy Surprise Inside!"

That's what it says on the side of every box of Cracker Jack, and that positioning strategy is what makes Cracker Jack different from its competitors. Other companies may produce a similar product but nobody else puts a toy inside of every box. Every box of Cracker Jack has included a toy since F.W. Rueckheim came up with the idea eighty years ago.

If you are to keep pace in today's ever-changing business environment, you must discover, accept, develop and capitalize on a position in your market that is as simple and clearly defined as Cracker Jack's position in snack food. And you must find a way to communicate that position that is as clear and dramatic as Cracker Jack's "Toy Surprise Inside!" The process is positioning strategy.

Cracker Jack's positioning strategy

The development of Cracker Jack shows how the process works. F.W. Rueckheim moved to Chicago after the great fire of 1871 and went into the popcorn business. He was very successful, and his brother Louis emigrated from Germany to join him. In 1893 Chicago's first world's fair, the Columbian Exposition, was held. The Rueckheim brothers had a prime location in the middle of the fair. Many people would be selling popcorn so they decided to develop a new product. F.W. had purchased some candy-making equipment, and Louis used that equipment to create a confection of popcorn mixed with peanuts and covered in molasses.

The new product was a tremendous success at the fair. Legend has it that a salesman tried the new snack food and exclaimed: "That's a cracker jack!" F.W. agreed, trademarked the name, and "Cracker Jack" it's been ever since.

Cracker Jack's popularity grew rapidly. In 1910 the company began putting a coupon on each box. You could save your coupons and send them to Chicago in exchange for a prize. In 1912 F.W. made the decision that gives Cracker Jack its unique position. He abandoned the coupon and put the prize *inside* the box.

Cracker Jack is now a division of the Borden company with a well-defined market position. When you buy a box of Cracker Jack, you know you'll receive a quality candy-coated popcorn product mixed with peanuts. And there'll be a prize in every box. There's no confusion. Cracker Jack remains a clear and uncomplicated choice. Because it holds that position, Cracker Jack commands a premium price over its competitors.

Personal experience

As a positioning strategist, I help new and existing businesses discover, accept, develop and capitalize on unique positions, crackerjack positions, in the marketplace.

My background gives me a perspective that helps others see their situations from the market's point of view. I've flown jet planes, been a newspaper reporter and served as a bank director. I've sold advertising, commercial real estate and bootleg whiskey. I've developed and administered a management services division for a billion-dollar, multi-state corporation.

I've managed, owned and supervised broadcast properties, including radio and television stations. I've also managed and leased space in shopping centers and office buildings. I've prepared tax returns for H&R Block and taken campers on horseback rides in the Rocky Mountains. I've even been a lifeguard.

I've taught sales training seminars throughout the country and been a business, convention and association speaker in 26 states. I've been a television news announcer and a country music disc jockey. I've met Marilyn Monroe, George Bush and Willie Nelson.

And through it all I've come to see that businesses and people are successful when they establish unique positions and develop strategies to support those positions.

Positioning strategy requires good judgment

Good judgment comes from experience. Experience comes from bad judgment.

Experience that comes from other people's bad judgment is much less painful than experience that comes from your own. This book is based on good and bad experiences. It includes my experiences, and those of my clients and others I've either observed or researched. Studying these experiences will help you make the positioning strategy decisions only you can make.

It's up to you

Developing a positioning strategy is important because your fate is in your hands and yours alone. There's not much help out there.

The divorce rate and scattering of families across the country mean many of us can no longer rely on our families for support and guidance. The failure of Lyndon Johnson's Great Society and War on Poverty taught us that we can't depend on the U.S. Government to look after us either. The flurry of corporate takeovers, bankruptcies and subsequent reorganizations destroyed our belief that major corporations would always be there for us. So it's up to you.

And you have to deal with a world evolving at an ever-increasing rate. If you hope to keep up with constant change, you must narrow your focus to an area you can manage. You do that by discovering, accepting, developing and capitalizing on your unique position in your market. Crackerjack positioning will help you do that.

Crackerjack positioning defined

Let's start with a couple of definitions:

> **crack-er-jack,** *n.* a person or thing of striking excellence.

> **po-si-tion-ing,** *v.t.* putting in a particular location or condition of advantage.

Therefore, **"crackerjack positioning"** is the act of putting a person or enterprise of striking excellence in a marketplace location or condition of advantage.

That's what this book is about, placing your crackerjack capabilities in a position of advantage — a *position that is then clearly communicated to your target market.*

The process

First you discover what your capabilities are, then you find a spot in your part of the marketplace where you can position those capabilities. Once you've located that hole, you develop a strategy to capture and secure the position. Next you put the strategy into effect, tinker with it as need be, and you'll soon own a crackerjack position. Not only will you own the position, it will be virtually impossible for someone to take it from you unless you abandon it.

The process is simple to understand but not easy to accomplish. It's like playing par golf. All you have to do to play par golf is hit the green in regulation and never take more than two putts to sink the ball. Simple process, difficult to master.

Mastering the simple process of crackerjack positioning is worth the trouble. When you operate from a crackerjack position, you'll be more productive with less effort because you're focused on a smaller area.

Being focused on a smaller area is a key element in crackerjack positioning because it's impossible to predict what's going to happen.

Accurate prediction is impossible

Market action often defies knowledgeable predictions. Look at the computer market. In 1978 several research organizations forecast what the size of the personal computer market would be in 1985. The most optimistic prediction estimated a $2 billion market. The market actually surpassed $25 billion.

Just as you can't predict what's going to happen in the marketplace, you also can't predict or control what your competition is going to do about whatever happens. You can be sure your competition isn't just going to sit around while you take over the market. It's amazing how many people seem to believe they can throw a hand grenade into the enemy camp and their foe will just stand there and applaud. That's highly unlikely. The best you can do is better the odds in favor of your success. Crackerjack positioning will help you improve those odds.

Cross-checking improves the odds

Narrowing the odds to establish a crackerjack position requires constant cross-checking of several factors. These factors are:

1. Personal Strengths
2. Company Strengths
3. Market Position
4. Competition
5. Market Trends

Cross-checking, by itself, is not enough. It's your *interpretation* of the information the cross-checking reveals that makes the difference. That interpretation and the actions you take as a result give you your position in the marketplace.

Cross-checking market indicators is like flying with only instruments in an airplane. When a pilot can't see the ground because of bad visibility due to weather, she must rely on what her instruments tell her to safely fly the plane. A pilot uses six basic instruments to determine what the airplane's attitude is and to ensure that she is flying on the right course. No single instrument tells the pilot the plane's attitude at a given moment by itself. It's the pilot's interpretation of the relationship of the information those instruments provide that tells her what's happening. The pilot must constantly cross-check the instruments and interpret the results to safely navigate through the clouds.

So it is with navigating through today's murky marketplace. No one element will tell you what to do. It takes a cross-check of all the factors coupled with your interpretation of how those factors affect your enterprise. You're the one who has to interpret the indicators. You can get help and support from other sources, but in the final analysis you're flying the plane.

The world grows increasingly complex

The world grows more complex by the minute. An M.I.T. study says that available information has increased six hundred times in the last ten years. No one can keep pace with that rate of increase.

Not only is the total amount of information increasing at a geometric rate, consumers are becoming more demanding. That demand is fracturing markets into ever-smaller pieces. Companies scramble to keep up. Ten years ago the average supermarket stocked 9,000 items. Today it carries over 30,000. Revlon offers 158 shades of lipstick. Even Coca-Cola, which was represented for almost 100 years by a single taste now bottles several flavors in a variety of sizes.

Television viewing choices

Look what's happened in television. In most markets today you have a choice of thirty, forty or fifty viewing options. It wasn't always that way.

Early television viewing came from one or two stations. Major markets might have as many as four. Stations carrying programs from the three major networks only had to be concerned with each other.

Then came cable television. Community Antenna Television (CATV) systems were originally constructed to bring network television viewing to rural or mountainous areas. As television viewers became more sophisticated, they demanded more viewing options. Satellites made it possible to transmit programming signals around the world. Soon cable systems were being constructed in major markets to satisfy audience demands. Ted Turner made arrangements for cable systems to carry his independent Atlanta television station. Network stations complained, but in vain, for the viewer would not be denied. Soon specialized cable networks formed, providing a plethora of viewing options.

Now you can choose a pitchman peddling a wok, a half-naked woman whispering sweet nothings into her lover's ear, or a preacher expounding about the sins of whispering sweet nothings. You can watch news as it happens around the world. If you're still not satisfied, you can stop by the corner video store and rent a movie to watch on your VCR. Your viewing choices are now infinite.

This explosion of viewing alternatives leaves network television stations with a problem. Ten years ago the three network television stations controlled ninety-one percent of prime time viewing. Today, network stations command less than 65 percent and their audience share continues to shrink.

Specialization enhances credibility

Each time a new programming specialty is developed, the major networks lose another part of their audience. Consumers perceive that the specialist will out-perform the generalist in the specialist's area of expertise. Consumers don't go to a general practitioner for brain surgery.

The market perception is generally correct. When the Challenger space shuttle blew up, CNN, the news specialist, was the only network providing live coverage of the launch. During the war in the Persian Gulf, CNN was considered the credible news source with up-to-the-minute information.

No matter what promotions or advertising the networks run, they'll never recapture this lost audience. They'll have to adjust to the changing market or go the way of the dinosaur.

Market fragmentation is universal

Every profession and industry is faced with the same fragmentation. It's simply impossible to continue to attempt to be all things to all people and succeed. If a business is to keep pace with increasing competition and the information explosion, it must specialize. It must not only specialize, it must communicate that specialty in a dramatic way.

Developing a crackerjack position and learning to communicate that position in a dramatic way require a creative approach. A creative approach comes from looking at your situation from different perspectives. Different perspectives come from expanding your mind. So let's expand your mind.

Color
Outside
The Lines

Studies show that children are highly creative. They maintain an open mind and develop resourceful solutions to problems. A five-year-old boy's pet frog fell into a shaft in his back yard. The boy's father tried to free the frog. He used a stick, then a shovel, finally trying to reach the frog with tongs. Nothing seemed to work. Finally the boy said, "Dad, can I try?" The father answered, "Sure, Son, go ahead." The boy picked up a water hose attached to a nearby faucet, turned the water faucet on and proceeded to fill the hole with water. As the hole filled, the frog rose to the top, where it was easily rescued.

Most children have lost that creative ability by the age of nine because their families and the American education system have convinced them they must conform if they are to fit into society. The blackest day in a child's life is the day he or she is finally convinced they must color *inside* the lines. They have established their first paradigm. Paradigms make it difficult to develop a unique crackerjack positioning strategy.

The restrictions of paradigm thinking

Paradigm comes from the Greek root "paradeigma," which means "model or pattern." It's the atmosphere in which we live. Our paradigm is to us like water is to fish.

Each of us creates our own paradigm. We do that by interpreting the messages we receive from the world. We have an experience, receive a message, interpret that message and establish a new paradigm based on our interpretation. Sometimes the paradigm limits us to a greater degree than is necessary.

Mark Twain said: "We should be careful to get out of an experience only the wisdom that is in it . . . and stay there, lest we be like the cat that sits down on a hot stove-lid. She will never sit down on a hot stove-lid again . . . and that is well; but also she will never sit down on a cold one any more."

Each of us has "Don't sit on *any* stove-lid" rules in our paradigm. And these rules limit our perspective.

Businesses operate within paradigms

Industries and professions have the same problem. Their paradigms are made up of the collective thinking and beliefs of the participants in that industry founded on years of experience.

Industry paradigms include "Don't sit on *any* stove-lid" rules. These rules mean that major new technical developments in an industry often come from someone beyond its borders. Insiders are limited by the boundaries of their paradigms. Outsiders aren't. If you are to establish a new position in your industry, you've got to get beyond your present paradigm.

The classic nine-dot puzzle

The puzzle demonstrates both what must be done and how difficult it is to do it. Look at these nine dots and follow the instruc-
tions.

•   •   •

•   •   •

•   •   •

Connect all nine dots in the above drawing using no more than
four straight lines, and do not lift your pencil from the paper.

Give yourself a few minutes to try to solve this puzzle before
going on to read the answer.

Think outside the dots

The puzzle is impossible to solve if you assume that there is an
imaginary fence around the nine dots beyond which you cannot
extend your lines. Most people make this assumption. Therefore,
a boundary exists in the mind of the problem solver that's not part
of the problem. She is limited by her self-constructed paradigm.

When this artificial restraint is lifted, there are many solutions to the problem. The following one is the most common.

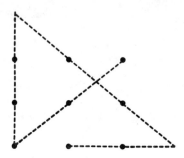

Other solutions include making the dots bigger so you can connect them with three lines. One person folded the paper in such a way that the dots could be connected with one line. A young girl said she could also do it with one line . . . but you must have a pencil with a very large lead, a lead wide enough to cover the entire nine dots.

When you maintain an open mind, you eliminate imagined restraints. There's no limit to what you can do when you get outside the paradigm.

Howard Head thought outside the dots

Howard Head did not restrict his paradigm. He consistently broke meaningless rules and got outside the nine dots.

Head was an aircraft design engineer during World War II. Following the war he began snow skiing. Head soon became frustrated with his inability to master the sport and began to question the quality and design of ski equipment.

Most of us do that. When we're having difficulty mastering a sport, we blame the equipment. Unlike most of us, however, Head did something about it. Relying on his aircraft design experience,

Head believed he could build better skis out of aircraft material than what was currently being built.

The existing paradigm in the skiing industry at that time said that nothing was superior to the hickory ski. It was the accepted truth. No industry expert thought of questioning that truth.

Head was not an industry expert. He was an outsider. So Head challenged the industry paradigm. He designed and perfected the Head metal ski. Head metal skis rapidly became the standard and revolutionized skiing.

Soon the Head Ski Company was the largest manufacturer of quality recreational skis in the world. Head found that he had neither the interest nor the talent to run a large business so he sold his company to AMF for $16 million and retired to an estate outside Baltimore, Maryland.

Head and tennis

Head took up a new sport — tennis. Once again he became frustrated with his success and once again he questioned the equipment. Head mulled over the problem. For two years he tinkered with racket design. Nothing worked.

At 3:00 one morning, Head awoke suddenly. The answer was clear. Make the racket BIGGER. Head checked the rules to see if that was permitted. There were some limitations on how the racket could be strung. Otherwise the rule simply stated: "The racket is the implement used to strike the ball." You could hit the ball with a barn door if you could figure out how to swing it.

Tennis rackets were originally made of wood. Wood was the only material available. Wood construction limited the racket's size. If you made the wooden racket bigger, it would be either fragile and easily broken or heavy so that you couldn't swing it comfortably. Hence the traditional size and shape.

Modern material had been used to make rackets before Howard Head invented the Prince. Metal rackets were common. However, like the wooden rackets, they were the traditional size and shape.

The power of paradigm thinking

Companies manufacturing metal rackets, including the Head division of AMF, were not stupid. The manufacturers were simply locked into the accepted thinking. No one thought to change the racket's size.

Head said that the invitation to innovate went unanswered because the traditional geometry was so fixed in people's minds that it just never occurred to anyone that bigger might be better.

Once Head found that the rules did not limit the size of the racket, he designed the Prince racket. The Prince is two inches wider and three inches longer than the traditional racket. More important, the "sweet spot," that area where the ball can be hit with the greatest amount of control, delivers twenty percent more power and is four times as large in the Prince as in the average racket.

As more and more tennis players grow up playing with the Prince, experts believe that the large racket will become the standard. Once again Howard Head revolutionized a sport.

Like Howard Head, you have to expand beyond the paradigm of accepted thinking to create a new position.

Think beyond the paradigm

One approach is to adopt the perspective of an alien suddenly placed on this planet. Assume that you know everything about man and society except what has been done in the past by other companies to solve a particular problem. You question existing premises and take a different tack. As an alien you are willing to ask the dumb questions that will provide new solutions.

The merchant's daughter

The English fable of the merchant's daughter and the pebbles illustrates the value of taking a different perspective when looking at a problem to be solved.

The story took place in England at a time when it was still

possible to imprison people who were deeply in debt. A merchant had run up a sizable obligation to a very ugly and unattractive moneylender. The moneylender desired the merchant's daughter so he offered a bargain. He would cancel the debt in exchange for the daughter's hand in marriage.

Both the merchant and his daughter were appalled at the offer. So the moneylender suggested an alternative. He would select two pebbles from the path, a white one and a black one. He would place the pebbles in a small sack and the daughter would then reach into the sack and blindly select a pebble.

If she selected the white pebble, the moneylender would cancel the debt and the daughter would remain free. If she selected the black pebble, the moneylender would cancel the debt but the daughter would have to marry him. If she refused to select either pebble, the merchant would be jailed and the daughter would starve.

The merchant and the daughter had no alternative so they reluctantly agreed to the bargain.

The moneylender reached down to the path and picked up two pebbles. Terrified at the possible outcome, the daughter was still alert enough to see the moneylender place two black pebbles into the bag. What to do?

Her obvious alternatives were to:

1. Expose the moneylender as a fraud, in which case he would be furious and would throw the merchant in jail.
2. Refuse to take a pebble, which would have the same result.
3. Take a black pebble and sacrifice herself for her father.

The daughter had three equally unattractive choices, each based on the assumption that the outcome would be determined by the color of the pebble she selected. But the daughter looked at the problem from a different perspective, from outside the nine dots, and discovered a fourth option.

The daughter reached into the sack, withdrew a pebble and, displaying great nervousness at the possible outcome of this exercise, immediately fumbled it onto the path below, where it was lost among all the other pebbles.

"How clumsy of me," she said, "but all is not lost. We can determine the color of the pebble I chose by looking at the color of the pebble remaining in the bag."

Since the pebble remaining in the bag was black, and since the moneylender was not about to admit his dishonesty, the debt was forgiven and the daughter went free.

The daughter went free because she thought beyond the nine dots, beyond the apparent limits of the problem, and came up with an alternative solution. Because of the moneylender's dishonest actions, the daughter's creative solution put her in a position where she could not fail.

Solutions from outside the accepted paradigm often do that. Howard Head's decision to build a bigger racket was both simple and revolutionary. It opened up a new perspective on the entire sport.

Arriving at new solutions and alternative positions is not that difficult once you develop the habit. You may not invent a bigger tennis racket but you can expand your thinking with practice.

Use creativity to modify the square

Consider a square illustrated by four lines on a sheet of paper, each line the same length and joined together at the corners in perfect 90-degree angles.

Now what can you do with that square to make it different? How about extending all the lines an equal amount and making the square larger? Or you could shorten the lines and make it smaller.

You could add something to it, like a large A in the middle. Or add something else, say, a $ sign.

You can subtract part of the area encompassed by the square if you take one line, break it in two, extend both lines and join them in the area previously encompassed by the square. You can duplicate the square and multiply the number available. Or you can divide it into four smaller squares.

You can combine it with a different design, say, a triangle. You can change its color or its position. How about adding a third dimension and making it a cube?

By simply studying a square, you can come up with a number of alternative ways of displaying it. And it doesn't take long either. All you have to do is expand your mind to consider other possibilities.

Five-sensing

Another approach to developing solutions is to look at the problem utilizing all five senses: sight, sound, taste, touch and smell. Look at your situation. How can you improve it using each sense?

Five-sensing dramatically expands what can be done in any situation. Focusing on each sense provides a new and entirely different perspective. New perspectives expand your mind.

Feed your mind

Your mind must be fed before it can be expanded. You feed your mind by going to art galleries, bookstores and libraries. You also expand your thinking by attending movies and plays, particularly ones that are out of your main stream of thinking.

Ideas are everywhere. They will explode from your mind when you challenge it by expanding your paradigm.

Most of us are socially incestuous. We have lunch and spend time with people in the same business we are in, people we see every day. These associations lead us to think alike, to live in a common paradigm.

So have lunch with people from a totally different environment. Take a professor to lunch. Meet psychologists and doctors and bankers. Take them to lunch and listen.

Challenge your mind by reading material beyond your usual interests. Read short stories and poems and essays.

Use word-association

Word-association exercises provide a new perspective, particularly when your mind is active and challenged by new areas of interest.

Stop reading for a moment. Pick up the dictionary you always keep beside you when you're reading. Open it at random. Scan the page. Select a word that stimulates your thinking and then examine your situation with that word in mind.

I've just opened my dictionary to page 450, and my word is "magnet."

This dictionary defines "magnet" as:

1. a piece of iron, steel, or lodestone that has the property of attracting iron or steel, etc.
2. a person or thing that attracts.

As I apply that word to my current project, which is writing this book, "magnet" reminds me that I must keep you in mind and use stories and examples that will *attract* your interest.

"Attracting your interest" means I've got to avoid my usual tendency to tell you how to make a watch because you merely want to know what time it is. I won't always avoid that tendency but "magnet" reminds me to keep it under control.

Keep feeding your mind so you'll get in the habit of looking at opportunities from more than one perspective. New perspectives remind you that you don't have to color inside the lines.

Fill Your Medicine Pouch

Harry Jackson, the sculptor, developed a realistic yet unique style that is highly respected in the art world. Jackson's most famous work is a statue of John Wayne portraying his Academy Award-winning character of Rooster Cogburn in *True Grit.* A picture of that statue appeared on the cover of *Time* magazine when Wayne won the Oscar.

Several years ago Jackson displayed his work at the Gilcrease Museum in Tulsa, Oklahoma. He delivered a lecture at the Gilcrease when his show opened. During the talk Jackson explained how he researches a project before he begins sculpting.

Jackson uses a process he learned from the Indians. When Indians are faced with a problem, they collect all the pertinent information about the problem and let it sit in their minds. They call this process "putting the information in the medicine pouch." In due time a solution evolves.

Jackson follows the same procedure.

If, for example, Jackson is commissioned to do a statue of a particular Indian, he will research the Indian, the tribe, the environment, the dress, everything relating to that Indian. This sometimes results in a stack of material five feet high. Jackson then studies the material. He "puts it in his medicine pouch."

When he feels ready, Jackson sculpts the piece. He never refers to the research material again. As Jackson says, "The piece must be authentic but it must be my interpretation of the material, not simply a copy of the research."

And so it is with you. Your crackerjack positioning decisions should come from your "medicine pouch," where you combine the information you collect with the wisdom derived from your unique experiences. The result will be realistic and authentic, yet unique. To achieve that result you need to fill your medicine pouch.

Collecting information is a messy process

It's messy because, just as there are no absolutely correct instruments in instrument flying, there are no absolutely accurate research sources.

You've just got to poke around and see what you can stir up. You never know when some helpful tidbit of information will appear, a tidbit that will clarify the direction you seek.

You'll know when your pouch is full

No one can tell you how much information is enough. There's no formula. Some books have checklists that could keep a forty-person research staff busy for years. Other ventures have been launched after one afternoon on the telephone.

You'll want enough information to give you a comfortable overview of the situation. The overview should tell you how large the market is, who's in it, how it got where it is, where it's going and how you might fit into it.

Filling your pouch to help you make a crackerjack positioning decision is similar to purchasing a new car or a major appliance. When you decide to make such a purchase, you generally have an idea what you want. You then begin visiting dealers to collect information. You may stick with your original notion or you may change your mind. The decision depends on the information you collect and your analysis of that information. Nobody can tell you how many dealers to visit. You simply interview dealers until you have enough information to be confident that the decision you are making is the correct one for you.

Collecting information leading to a crackerjack positioning decision follows the same process.

Let the medicine pouch work

When you have collected enough information to be comfortable that you've got an overview of the situation, then let the batch ferment in your medicine pouch until conclusions begin bubbling to the top.

An important part of the mixture is a knowledge of strengths, both yours and those associated with your enterprise, so we'll look at that next.

Dance With The One Who Brung You

If you are to achieve a position that is unique and will stand out from your competitors, that position must be built on your strengths, not your weaknesses. Valuable strengths are often overlooked because they are taken for granted. The tendency is to be more concerned about curing weaknesses than building on strengths. Following that road invites you to fall victim to the "all things to all people" syndrome.

Dance with the one who brung you

I've never seen the importance of building on strengths better described than it was by Coach Darrell Royal in 1969. Royal was head football coach at the University of Texas. His team had completed an undefeated season with a dramatic come-from-behind victory over the University of Arkansas in Fayetteville. If Texas were to become national champion, however, the team had to win one more game. Texas had to defeat Notre Dame in the Cotton Bowl on January 1, 1970.

The University of Texas team used the wishbone offense. The wishbone offense is heavily dependent on the run. Notre Dame's defense against the run was outstanding. Notre Dame had been able to hold their opponents to an average of less than eighty-five yards per game rushing. They had been able to achieve this record because the Notre Dame defensive line was huge. The Notre Dame defensive line outweighed Texas some thirty-five pounds per man.

Sportswriters kept asking Coach Royal what changes he was going to make to offset this disadvantage. Finally, at a press conference shortly before the game, Royal told them:

"We aren't going to change anything. We're going to do what we've been doing all season long. We're going to dance with the one who brung us."

And the score of the game was Texas 21, Notre Dame 17.

Coach Royal knew that to be successful you must build on your strengths and not be concerned about your weaknesses. His team focused on what they did well and emerged victorious.

Lincoln built on strengths

Abraham Lincoln recognized the importance of building on strengths. Lincoln's staff told him that General Ulysses S. Grant, commander of the Union forces, was a drunkard. Lincoln's reply was that they should find out what brand of liquor General Grant drank and then send a case of it to each of the other generals.

Lincoln knew that Grant's strength was winning battles. The fact that Grant drank was not important unless his drinking interfered with his ability to win battles. Grant's drinking didn't do that so Lincoln ignored it.

Success is achieved by building on strengths, not correcting weaknesses. Success is achieved by "dancing with the one who brung you."

Each of us has a unique package of strengths

You possess a unique package of strengths, skills and capabilities that has never been housed in one human being before and will never be duplicated again. Just as no two sets of fingerprints have ever been the same, no two individuals have ever possessed identical talents.

Your unique package gives you the potential to become the crackerjack you were intended to be. And when your unique package is combined with the equally unique talents of your co-workers, your company has the capability to develop a singular position in the marketplace.

Unfortunately the potential locked into this bundle of unique strengths is often overlooked. Walt Disney said, "The more you are like yourself, the less you are like anybody else, and that is what makes you unique. Yet the world is full of duplicates and has very few originals."

Strengths often taken for granted

Your strengths come from your raw talent. Your raw talent is what makes you yourself. Yet these talents, these potential strengths, are often ignored. They are ignored because they are taken for granted. They're taken for granted because our basic raw talent comes to us easily. We live in a society built on the Puritan work ethic. Such a society says that if it doesn't hurt, it has no value. Our raw talent comes to us easily so we discount these skills and conclude they have no value. "No pain, no gain" becomes our credo.

Yet what our hand naturally turns to can be a powerful ally in our effort to become the crackerjack we were intended to be. In our bundle of strengths is the potential to discover and develop our unique position, the position we must have if we're to survive in today's constantly fragmenting marketplace. In our hearts we know this, but our Puritan ethic still makes us turn away. We can't escape the belief that anything that is not painful to master does not have value. After all, if we can do it, anybody can do it, and therefore this is not a marketable strength. So we expend valuable time and energy looking elsewhere.

"Acres of Diamonds"

Russell Conwell pointed out the fallacy in this reasoning in his famous lecture, "Acres of Diamonds." Conwell presented the talk over six thousand times and founded Temple University with the proceeds. In his talk, Conwell emphasized that opportunity lies in our own back yard. He told the story of a man who sold his home and traveled the world seeking his fortune, only to return and find that his former house was located on acres of diamonds. Too late, Conwell's hero realized he didn't have to look elsewhere for his fortune; it was right beneath his feet.

And you don't have to look elsewhere for your strengths either. You simply have to recognize and accept the potential in the capabilities you already possess.

We often fail to recognize the power that exists in the strengths, skills and capabilities we already possess. And in failing to recognize that potential, we overlook our most advantageous starting point in developing a positioning strategy.

Companies also take strengths for granted

Companies can fall victim to the same malady. They'll develop a strong position built on their unique talents, then undermine their own efforts by stretching their resources to do things they're less suited for. They'll take from the strength to feed a weakness.

American Motors took from its strengths to feed its weaknesses. American Motors owned a strong and profitable position as the leader in four-wheel-drive vehicles. American Motors had the Jeep. Instead of focusing on that virtually uncontested position, American Motors chose to take Jeep profits and throw them into a hopeless passenger car battle with General Motors, Ford and Chrysler. Ultimately American Motors exhausted its resources and vanished into Chrysler.

International Falls builds on reputation

The concept of capitalizing on strengths applies to cities as well as companies and individuals. International Falls, Minnesota, is often reported as the coldest spot in the lower forty-eight states. For years the residents defended their city against jokes and gibes about its awful weather. And then the community decided to change that perceived weakness into a strength.

The city now calls itself "The Nation's Icebox." To prove their claim, civic leaders installed the world's largest thermometer in Smokey Bear Park. The thermometer can register temperatures as low as 60 below zero. The $17,000 thermometer proudly displays the lowest official temperature ever recorded in the city, minus 46, which occurred in January 1968.

Civic leaders urge corporations to bring their new products to International Falls for testing. And the strategy is working. Several products, including Sears Roebuck & Co.'s DieHard batteries and RJR Nabisco Inc.'s Cream of Wheat, have appeared in television commercials with International Falls' frozen landscape as a backdrop. Research teams from Japan, Sweden and England, as well as the United States, now come to International Falls to test their products during the winter season. A perceived weakness has been turned into a strength, and International Falls is now capitalizing on its unique position in the marketplace.

Indianapolis focuses on sports

Indianapolis, Indiana, is another city that has become successful by building on strengths. The city already hosted one of the world's most famous sporting events, the Indianapolis 500 auto race. The city fathers decided to build on this base and capitalize on the state's fanaticism with sports.

Indianapolis built the $80 million Hoosier Dome in the downtown area and attracted the Baltimore Colts. The Dome is an excellent example of private and public interests focusing on developing a unique position. Private interests contributed $30 million toward the Dome's construction, and voters approved a one percent food-and-beverage tax for the public contribution.

Other national sports events have followed the Colts in Indianapolis, and the city is now called the "Amateur Sports Capital" of the country.

A crackerjack position created by discovering, accepting, developing and capitalizing on one's unique strengths is just as successful for individuals as it is for cities and business organizations.

Discovering strengths is simple but not easy

Discovering strengths upon which to build a positioning strategy is simple because the best opportunity is generally obvious. It's not easy because the strength that may be obvious to an outside observer is difficult for you to see when you are blinded by myriad daily business demands. It's also easy to overlook a strength because you work with it on a daily basis. In the process you've become familiar with it. And as Publilius Syrus said in his *Maxims*, "Familiarity breeds contempt." (Mark Twain added " . . . and children," but that's another matter.)

The New Coke debacle

The Coca-Cola Company's experience in 1985 shows what can happen when you are too close to your strengths to see their value. Pepsi-Cola had been running blind taste tests comparing Pepsi-Cola and Coca-Cola since 1975. In test after test participants chose Pepsi-Cola over Coca-Cola, albeit by a slim margin. The Coca-Cola Company became obsessed with developing a new formula that would beat Pepsi-Cola in these tests. The company was so focused on developing a new product it overlooked the strength it already possessed.

Coca-Cola Company executives were ecstatic when they finally developed a drink that test participants preferred over Pepsi. They were so ecstatic they decided to replace original Coke with this new formula. The Coca-Cola Company researched the market extensively before it made this decision but it did not ask consumers how they would feel if the drink they had been accustomed to for almost 100 years was removed from the market altogether. By not asking that question the Coca-Cola Company failed to recognize that a significant part of original Coke's true strength came from being considered as integral a part of American culture as the Statue of Liberty, apple pie and motherhood. People might prefer the taste of the new formula but taste was only one part of Coke's image. Overwhelming public reaction called the Coca-Cola Company's attention to this fact and original Coke quickly returned to the market as Classic Coke.

If the world's largest soft drink company with all its research capability can miss the true strength of its leading product, you can see why it is so difficult for each of us to see our own core strengths. It's virtually impossible to do it by yourself, so get help.

Architects build on strengths

One of my clients is an architectural firm. The partners in this firm wanted to create dramatic projects that would appear on the cover of *Architectural Digest*. They entered contests, bid on exotic projects and accepted unprofitable contracts to remodel houses in order to display their creativity. Nothing seemed to work.

However, along the way the firm had built on the partners' innate strengths and developed an ability to design projects requiring skilled architectural work to be performed on a low budget within demanding restrictions on tight deadlines. I asked them if this wasn't an unusual talent. They said that they didn't think so. This kind of work was easy for them. Surely anybody could do it.

Market surveys verified that the firm was perceived as being very good at designing journeyman architectural projects under budget and within deadlines. In fact, they were so highly regarded in this area that another architectural firm hired my client to do work the first firm couldn't get out. We also found that other firms couldn't do this work. Not only that, when competitive firms found out that my client was being considered for a project that met these tight restrictions, the competitive firm often dropped out and did not submit a bid.

So the partners decided to quit pursuing work that experience had taught them they weren't going to get anyway. The firm chose, instead, to focus on the work they did well.

The first year this practice was in effect became the best year in the firm's history. Even better, the firm booked enough business that first year to carry them through the following year as well. They soon outgrew their office space and now have a firm three times the size, all because they focused on their strengths and ignored their weaknesses.

Whatever your enterprise, building on strengths rather than focusing on weaknesses is the cornerstone to successful cracker-jack positioning. So dance with the one who brung you.

How To Find Your Partner

For several years I've presented a motivational talk entitled "You Gotta Dance With Who Brung You!" The talk is based on the concepts outlined in the last chapter. Often people will come up to me after the talk and say, "Don, I'd like to dance with the one who brung me, but I don't know who that it is. How do I find out what my strengths are?"

Finding strengths is not the problem

A myriad of books are available with exercises to help you find your strengths, your partner. Three resources you might consider are *Know Your Own Mind* by James Greene and David Lewis, published by Rawson Associates; *Do What You Love, The Money Will Follow* written by Marsha Sinetar, published by Dell; and *DO IT!* by John-Roger and Peter McWilliams, published by Prelude Press. Each book takes a slightly different perspective to help you with your search for strengths. All three are available in paperback editions.

The problem is not finding strengths, it's recognizing and accepting the strengths once you've found them. You may need outside help to achieve that result.

My stepfather was an interior decorator. He was also slightly color blind. Sometimes a client would bring in a multi-colored piece of fabric and ask him to match the green in it. He would look at the fabric but couldn't see the green so he would ask her to point it out. When the client physically pointed to the color, he was able to see it. This apparent weakness was actually a strength because it enabled my stepfather to develop creative color combinations that people with normal vision might not see. First, however, he needed outside help to find the color. So it is with us. We need outside support to help us focus on our strengths so we can develop them.

"Lighten up" to find strengths

It's also difficult to see our strengths when we take ourselves too seriously. When we take ourselves too seriously, we create barriers that keep us from recognizing and accepting the strengths we possess.

Let's face it. Not everyone is put on this earth to discover penicillin. Nor is everyone called to be Winston Churchill and lead his country to victory in a battle for survival. Each person, however, is put here with the talent to make a unique contribution that only she can make.

The traditional "Serenity" prayer provides a perspective for locating, accepting and developing our strengths.

"'God grant me the serenity to accept the things I cannot change, the courage to change the things I *can* change, and the wisdom to know the difference.'"

In short, "Lighten up!"

A "lighten up" attitude is a crucial requirement if your search for strengths is to be successful. The following matrix shows why a relaxed, judicious approach to the quest is required.

Learning, doing matrix

The matrix premise is that each of our individual talents, skills or capabilities falls into one of the following quadrants:

Difficult To Do Difficult To Learn	Difficult To Do Simple To Learn
Simple To Do Difficult To Learn	Simple To Do Don't Remember Learning

Study the matrix, then answer this question: In which quadrant do the skills, talents and capabilities fall, upon which society places the greatest value?

Most people believe that society places the greatest value on the skills found in the "Difficult To Do, Difficult To Learn" quadrant. This is the usual answer because our culture is very serious. Remember the "no pain, no gain" credo? "Difficult To Do, Difficult To Learn" skills are the ones our culture says are the most valuable.

In reality, our most precious skills, our unique capabilities, are found in the "Simple To Do, Don't Remember Learning" quadrant. Because these skills and talents are uniquely ours, they are simple for us to do and we don't remember learning how to do them.

Pleasure comes from using strengths

In order to accept our strengths, we'll have to forget the message of our Puritan heritage. Suppose there are two girls who are baby sitters. The first girl loves baby sitting. The second girl hates it. Puritan doctrine says that the one who hates to baby sit is more virtuous because enjoyment is a sin. Yet this belief is inconsistent with the way we were created by our Higher Power.

In order to survive we must eat, so we are designed in such a way that eating is a pleasure. We must sleep, so sleeping is enjoyable. If our species is to avoid extinction, we must procreate; therefore, sex is enjoyable, particularly when love is involved. It follows, then, that we are constructed in such a way that the use of our unique talents should also be enjoyable. What you enjoy doing is a clue to your strengths.

Strengths come easily

Consider what your hand turns to easily. What part of your business would you naturally gravitate to if you were not under some outside influence like a deadline or money pressure? If it were completely up to you, what would you do first?

Each of us will answer that question differently. We'll answer it differently even if we are in the same business or profession.

Every business has specialized opportunities

Consider accounting. People outside the field tend to consider accounting to be dull and routine, nothing more than adding numbers. Accountants, however, fill many different roles. They are more than everybody's grown-ups telling us what we can and cannot do. Several of my clients are certified public accountants. And they display a variety of strengths and talents in their chosen profession.

One is in accounting because she likes the neatness of balanced books. She isn't interested in new trends or tax complexities, she simply likes to make everything come out even. As you might suspect, her clients' books are seldom out of balance.

Another client would be perfectly happy if he never saw another tax return or balanced another set of books. What he likes is staying on top of the constant changes in his field. He wants to know what's happening and then write articles and columns about how to deal with the changes.

A third CPA client is an expert in a specific business classification, small municipalities. He reads their publications, attends their conventions and stays in touch with their problems. Fully informed, he provides the unique accounting services a small town requires.

Still another accountant client specializes in nonprofit organizations and their distinctive accounting requirements.

Accounting offers a variety of specialized opportunities for building on strengths. What's true about accounting is also true about the market you're considering, so you need to locate those strengths.

One way to find strengths

Think about your skills and strengths that fall in the "Simple To Do, Don't Remember Learning" quadrant. They're easy to overlook because they aren't painful. Since they're not painful, you take them for granted. "Simple To Do, Don't Remember Learning" skills don't wake you up at 3:00 in the morning. "Difficult To Do, Difficult To Learn" items do.

"Simple To Do, Don't Remember Learning" may be hard to recognize but you've had clues. Often the clues are ethereal and quickly vanish. Think about a moment in your life when everything just came together. You were fulfilled and content and proud of what you had done. Your "Simple To Do, Don't Remember Learning" talent was at work. If you're like me, instead of recognizing its value, you may have said, "Too good to be true," and quickly returned to struggling with those "Difficult To Learn, Difficult To Do" obstacles.

Let's see if we can't recapture some of those precious moments of fulfillment and find the strengths that created them. This next exercise will help.

You'll need seven blank index cards. On the front of each card, list an achievement that you felt good about, an experience that put fire in your belly or a smile on your face or gave you a contented feeling of satisfaction. It doesn't have to be a moment of high drama. In fact, it probably isn't. But it gives you a tingle when you think about it.

At first you might find it difficult to list seven achievements. Your parents and teachers probably taught you to be modest and not brag about your exploits so you've set them aside. It may take some time to first recall and then accept those seven experiences as achievements. Keep at it until you get seven. Consider all aspects of your life. Think about education, hobbies and extracurricular activities in addition to your business experiences.

Write each achievement on a single card. Then turn the card over and write a short paragraph describing what happened. Include the steps you went through to accomplish it. Then rank the cards in their order of importance to you. Now circle the word in each paragraph that best describes what made this a fulfilling experience.

Next, write a statement about yourself using the seven words you have circled. The statement doesn't have to be grammatically correct, nor does it have to make sense to anybody but you. You might write something like this: My most fulfilling experiences indicate that I like to carefully *analyze* a situation, then *create* a solution by *visualizing* what can be done that nobody else has done. Then I *write* about the solution before I *implement* it by doing most of the work *myself* through contact with *people.*

As you look over the paragraph you've written, can you begin to see any possibilities you may not have considered? Any old strengths that you've overlooked or downplayed? This exercise will help but chances are you'll still need outside help to make sure you aren't missing any strengths that could be critical elements in your crackerjack positioning strategy. It's almost impossible to pick out our strengths without outside help because our strengths are such an integrated part of our being that we can't see them.

It's hard to see strengths without help

When I began speaking publicly it was quickly apparent to the other members of my Toastmasters club that my calling was motivational talks.

There was impressive data to support that conclusion. I frequently entered Toastmasters serious speech contests and generally won. Three times I went to the International Speech Contest

Finals as one of the top nine speakers in the entire Toastmasters International organization. So it was clear that my speaking talent was inspirational and motivational talks.

But I didn't see it. Since motivational speaking came easily to me, I thought anybody could do it and it didn't have any value. Instead of accepting my "Simple To Do, Don't Remember Learning" talent, I went after a "Difficult To Learn, Difficult To Do" skill.

Ego gets in the way

It was too easy to be a motivational speaker so I decided to be a humorist.

I took courses on humor and bought books on the subject. I even read most of them. I listened to humorous tapes, watched television comedy programs and taught courses on the use of humor in public speaking.

For a while I tried to be Mark Twain. Then I took a shot at Will Rogers. No, that wasn't it, I thought, I must really be Johnny Carson. Maybe Jerry Clower. On and on I went, searching for my comedic style.

Charles Jarvis, Joe Griffith, Doc Blakely and Roy Hatten worked with me. They were members of the National Speakers Association and were established humorous speakers. All of these gentlemen were very supportive. At various times, each one listened to tapes of my talks and gave me his candid evaluation. And each one gently told me that I was a motivational speaker, not a humorist. I ignored that part of their evaluations.

Focusing on weakness results in mediocrity

What was the result of all this effort? I became a mediocre humorous speaker. Whereas I could prevail in a serious speech contest with little effort, it took me four years to finally win the Toastmasters state humorous speech contest.

Humorous speech contest winner or not, my audiences still pictured me as a motivational speaker. It didn't matter how many humorous stories I told. There were occasions when I didn't think I had a single motivational word in my entire talk, yet I was still perceived as a motivational speaker.

It was almost unanimous. The audiences. The Toastmasters. The speech contests. The NSA humorous speakers. Everybody agreed that I was a motivational speaker who could use humor to highlight his message. Everybody agreed but me.

Outside consultant helps

Finally, after years of struggling on the fringes of the speaking industry, I went to an outside consultant, Juanell Teague, who is a speaking industry consultant from Dallas. With Juanell's help I finally got the message.

Now everybody, including me, agrees that I'm a motivational speaker who does a good job of using humor to highlight his message. Motivational speaking comes easily to me and I don't remember learning how to do it; therefore, I had a very hard time accepting that it was a valuable skill.

See why you need outside help? And, even more important, see why you should listen to what outsiders tell you?

Outside help brings the objectivity needed to recognize what you or your enterprise is doing right. Sometimes what we're doing that's working is right under our noses but we still miss it.

The obvious answer is easily overlooked

Michael Vance is a creative-thinking consultant. Vance is past director of Idea and People Development at both Disneyland and Walt Disney World. He is also a former dean of Disney University, which trains Disney theme park employees. Vance tells a story about the difficulties airlines had getting passengers to fly in the 747 when the giant plane was first introduced. The plane was so much larger than existing aircraft that passengers were cautious about trying it. Not Vance. He chose to fly on the 747 because he knew that he'd get better service. There were a lot of flight attendants and not many passengers.

Playboy was the right choice

Vance and an associate were on a 747 flight one day when an incident occurred that demonstrates how easy it is to overlook what we're doing right. Vance's companion asked for a copy of *Playboy* magazine. The flight attendant indignantly said that copies of *Playboy* were not on board. Later during the flight, a different airline representative told Vance that the 747 flights used to carry *Playboy* but the airline had taken the magazine off. Vance asked why they dropped *Playboy* and the representative answered, "Because the passengers kept stealing all the copies."

Vance points out that if the passengers are stealing the magazine, it's obviously the right choice. It's what the passengers want. You don't take the magazine off, you put more copies on!

Too close to see the big picture

Unfortunately, this is not an unusual incident. And you can see how it happens. Here's an airline employee miles away from dealing directly with passengers. The 747 flights are losing money because of low passenger loads, and some supervisor tells our hero to see what he can do about cutting 747 flight expenses.

"Aha!" says the hero, as he spots those disappearing *Playboy* magazines. "I can cut that expense by not putting any copies of *Playboy* on the 747."

The sad thing is that our hero is just doing his job. His supervisor might even commend him for keeping such an eagle-eye on the expenses. In the meantime the airline marketing department is probably giving away flight bags, pens, playing cards, and no telling what else, trying to get passengers on the 747. Nobody has noticed that the passenger doesn't want all that other stuff. What the passenger wants is a copy of *Playboy*. See why you need an outsider?

Determine what you're doing right

If you're in business, you're doing something right or you wouldn't be here. Today's highly competitive business environment won't tolerate incompetence for long. So you'll want to find out what's working.

Again, it's almost impossible to determine your business's strengths and weaknesses without outside help. You need outside help not only because it will give you an objective analysis but also because a key source of information is your work force. Employees are often intimidated when asked delicate questions by management. However they'll speak freely with an outside consultant when they know that their confidentiality is protected.

You'll want to know what your employees think the company does well. It's also useful to find out what the employees believe you think is important in the operation. This information will help you formulate your strategy once you have determined your position.

Ask your employees for opinions

Here are some suggested questions for your employees:

1. What is the history of the company? How did it get started?
2. Why is the company a success? What has caused it to grow?
3. What does the company do best? Why is that what they do best?
4. What should the company discontinue doing? Why?
5. What should the company consider adding? Why?
6. Who is a typical customer? Why do they buy from the company?
7. Are all of the company's products and/or services compatible with each other?
8. What can the employee contribute that he or she isn't contributing?

9. What incidents come to mind that display what the
company does well or doesn't do well?

With this information from your employees, coupled with what
you've learned about your personal skills, you'll have the internal
information you need to begin to formulate your crackerjack
position. Now you need to see how you are perceived outside the
enterprise.

Shoot The Stars

Prior to the age of sophisticated electronic navigational equipment, ships and aircraft navigated by "shooting the stars." A navigator used an instrument called a "sextant" to measure the relative altitudes of celestial bodies. The relationship between the measurements determined the ship or aircraft position at the time the measurements were made.

You will also need to "shoot the stars" to find your present position. Instead of celestial bodies, you'll use people who are familiar with you and your enterprise. Their comments will give you your present position.

Go into the marketplace

You can't find your present position sitting in your office. You've got to get into the marketplace and talk to the people who know you and what you've done. But you can't do it all yourself.

Once again, I suggest you use an outside resource to help you. Such a resource can't take your role because your personal feel for the marketplace is critical. However, there are certain facets of your survey that are much better handled by an independent interviewer. You are seeking information about your business that many people are reluctant to tell you to your face, especially if they are your friends as well as business acquaintances.

Don't believe just your friends

Friends are nice. Sometimes too nice. They won't directly tell you what you need to know because they might hurt your feelings and jeopardize the relationship. However they'll tell a trusted stranger almost anything in order to help you improve.

One of my former clients is an interior decorating firm. Many of their patrons were close friends of the client in addition to being customers. When I surveyed the patrons/friends, they were very reluctant to be open and honest until they were assured that their anonymity would be protected. When the patrons/friends understood that their comments would not be directly attributed to them, they became very cooperative and helpful.

It's surprising what people will tell a third party about their relationship with a business that they will not tell the firm directly. Government surveys have shown, for example, that ninety-six percent of unhappy customers won't tell you they are dissatisfied. They will, however, tell eight to ten other people.

Unbiased viewpoint

It's also difficult for you or your employees to make this survey because you're too involved in the daily operation of the business. An outside source not involved in the day-to-day operation is more likely to get an objective perception of your operation because she will not get bogged down in the subtleties of your business. It's easy to overlook possible strengths when you know yourself and your operation too well.

Several years ago I read a market survey done for a restaurant. The market research firm had gone to a great deal of trouble to find out that the principal reason people went to restaurants was the food. That may seem obvious, yet it illustrates the problem. The restaurant was so close to its operation that it wasn't sure what brought customers. The owners thought the customers may be coming because of the decor, the prices, the service or the location. While all of those items were part of the reason, the food was far ahead of all other considerations in attracting customers.

It's easy to become confused. We are so close to the situation that we can't read it accurately. Our position may be so obvious that we believe it can't possibly be true, just as the restaurant found it difficult to believe that the quality and variety of its food were the principal customer attraction.

Today's complex society looks for elaborate answers. So we nit-pick, looking for subtle differences our customer completely overlooks. The consumer has neither the time nor the interest to notice these nuances.

When you look at a business other than your own, you can see how positions are perceived.

Consider grocery stores

Within a one-mile radius of my house are several stores that sell groceries. Each has a very different position in my mind. I do most of my grocery shopping at a jumbo supermarket less than a mile away. I shop there because I've learned that store generally has what I want and the prices are low. It helps that the store is close to my home.

The jumbo store emphasizes its warehouse, low-price image. The store does relatively little out-of-store advertising and features few of the traditional grocery specials. Instead they reinforce their low-price image with in-store promotion.

For example, one in-store exhibit consists of several grocery carts filled to capacity with identical items. All the items in each cart were purchased at a different competitive store. On each cart is a show card naming the store where the items were purchased and listing the total price. The actual sales ticket is in the cart itself. The last cart in the display contains the same items with a sales ticket showing the prices in the jumbo store. The total price is always substantially less than any of the other carts.

Broader selection

Whenever I want an item just a little out of the ordinary, such as frozen asparagus, I have to go someplace other than the jumbo store. I generally go to a store that is about a mile farther away. Experience has taught me that this store will have the item because its selection is greater. Experience has also taught me that the price will be higher.

This store does not have a clear position in my mind. Sometimes they push their wide selection. Sometimes it's their specials. Currently it's customer service. The store's lack of consistency leaves me confused. Because I'm confused, I don't know how I would describe the store to somebody else.

Dairy store is specialized

Another neighborhood store is much smaller and focuses on dairy products. Because this store specializes, my perception is that their milk and eggs are fresher and better than I'll find at other stores. Notice I didn't say that the products actually *are* fresher and better. That's my perception. Whatever the truth, my perception is my reality. We'll talk more about that in the next chapter.

The dairy store's products are priced about the same or a little less than the jumbo store. And I can get in and out of there quickly. So, if it's milk or eggs that I need, the dairy store is where I'll go. Because I perceive the dairy store products to be better than the jumbo supermarket brands and because the dairy store is not far out of my way, I seldom buy dairy items at the jumbo supermarket.

Being "convenient" is no longer enough

Also within the mile radius is a convenience store, a relatively small store with limited inventory whose principal focus is, or was, convenience. The convenience store used to be the only place you could get milk, eggs, cigarettes, etc., after typical business hours.

The store was open late hours, weekends and holidays. Today you can purchase milk and beer at gasoline stations, and even the jumbo supermarket is open twenty-four hours a day, every day of the year except Christmas. The market changed and so did the convenience store.

Nowadays we look to the convenience store for benefits beyond timely hours. Convenience stores sell gasoline and feature hot coffee and soft drinks. Today the primary convenience store customer comes in to get something to drink rather than to pick up necessities on the way home.

Each store has a position

Each of these stores has a position in my mind whether it wants one or not. Each gets business from me depending on my perception of how it can satisfy my immediate need. The jumbo supermarket gets most of my grocery shopping because it has a good selection at a low price and is virtually always open. I go to the second supermarket when I'm looking for something beyond the selection at the jumbo. The dairy store sells me dairy products, and I'll stop at the convenience store for gasoline and hot coffee.

Three of the four stores have a good handle on their position and their marketing strategy supports it. I'm confused about the second supermarket. It must also be confused because it keeps changing its strategy.

Frequent strategy changes are not wise

A weak strategy consistently followed is better than a constantly changing one. Consumers are slow to change buying habits and won't do so without strong motivation. If you keep changing your marketing strategy, the consumer never learns enough about your enterprise to be motivated to change.

For example, the last significant supermarket positioning change in my mind occurred when the jumbo supermarket opened its doors several years ago. The opening of a 60,000-

square-foot store is a major neighborhood event. Even so, I didn't immediately change my shopping routine. I'm a creature of habit and those habits are well entrenched. It takes a major upheaval to get me to change a familiar pattern. It was some time before I moved my shopping from a familiar yet relatively expensive store to the new jumbo supermarket.

The strength of existing patterns is one reason it's important to find out what your present position is in the minds of your prospects. If you can capitalize on an existing position, your task will be much easier. Trying to change your position in your prospect's mind is almost impossible to do.

Ask questions to determine your position

You find out what your position is by asking questions. If you are not yet in business and therefore have no market position, this exercise can still be valuable. Pick an enterprise that you think will be a major competitor if you choose to enter the market. Follow this procedure, using your potential competitor as the principal.

Start with a list of people to interview. Include the following:

1. Customers, both past and present.
2. Competitors.
3. Association executives who can give you the big picture for your business.
4. Financial institutions familiar with your business specialty.
5. Editors, publishers and/or writers knowledgeable in your field and where you fit.
6. Suppliers who deal with many firms in your business and know the relative strengths of each.

You need to know how these people perceive your position. Is your position clear in their minds or is it confused, like the second supermarket is in my mind?

What do they think you do best? How does that relate to others in the business?

Use open-ended questions

Make an outline of what you need to know and convert that
outline to a list of questions. It's important to remember that
you're not looking for quantitative information as much as quali-
tative information. This means that your questions will be open-
ended, which allows the respondents to express their answers in
their words. It'll make the answers difficult to tabulate, but it's
more important to get their perceptions than to try to make the
answers fit a graph.

Questions for customers

A questionnaire for past and present clients/customers will ask
the following:

1. How long have you been a client/customer of ABC?
2. How did you hear about them?
3. Why did you select them?
4. Do they do all of your work of this type?
5. What other firms/companies do you use?
6. What do you like *best* about their work?
7. What do you like *least* about their work?
8. Compared with other firms/companies you have
   used, what are ABC's advantages? Disadvantages?
9. Have you had any unsatisfactory experiences working with ABC?
10. Are there any other services you would like ABC to
    provide?
11. Would you recommend ABC to others?
12. How would you describe them to others?

The last question is the most significant. The answer to that
question is the one that will tell you what you really want to know,
which is how clear your position is in the minds of your customers.
The earlier questions are helpful because they stimulate thought
that helps the respondent answer the last question.

Questions for suppliers and peers

Questionnaires for suppliers and peers are similar. A typical questionnaire for a peer or competitor will ask the following:

1. Are you familiar with ABC?
2. Have you ever worked with them?
3. What do you think they do best?
4. What do you think are their weaknesses?
5. Compared with other similar companies you have worked with, what are ABC's advantages? Disadvantages?
6. Have you had any unpleasant experiences working with ABC?
7. How would you describe ABC to someone else?

And for a supplier:

1. How long have you worked with ABC?
2. How did your relationship begin?
3. What do you like *best* about their work?
4. What do you like *least* about their work?
5. Compared with similar firms/companies, what are the advantages of working with ABC? Disadvantages?
6. Have you had any unpleasant experiences working with ABC?
7. Are there any other services you would like ABC to provide?
8. Would you recommend ABC to others?
9. How would you describe them to somebody else?

Analyze the answers to these questions and you'll get a feel for your perceived position in the marketplace. Generally your present position will come as no great surprise. It's been your intimacy with your operation that has kept it hidden from you.

Market perception is reality

It's difficult to accept market perception as reality because we are used to looking at the market from our own perspective. As a sage said, "When your only tool is a hammer, every problem looks like a nail."

When we fail to recognize that the market's paradigm is different from our own, we react like one of the three men who were lost in the North Woods. One man was an engineer, the second was a psychologist, and the third a theologian. In attempting to find their way, the three men came upon a cabin and knocked on the door. There was no answer, but the door was open so they went in.

Once inside they saw a strange sight. A potbellied stove was wired to the rafters high in the cabin close to the roof. The stove's exhaust pipe went from the stove through a hole in the roof to release the smoke.

The men speculated on why the stove was installed in this manner.

"The answer is clear," said the engineer. "This trapper understands thermodynamics. He wired his stove to the rafters because he knows that he will get even heat distribution throughout the cabin from that location."

Whereupon the psychologist commented, "Your point is well taken but incorrect. Our trapper has been alone in the North Woods for years. He's lonely and wants to return to the security of his mother's womb. So he wired the stove to the rafters and sleeps under it to regain the warm feeling of being in the womb."

"Interesting," said the theologian. "But you are both mistaken. Man has looked upon fire as a symbol of a higher being for centuries, particularly when it's elevated. The stove is obviously the trapper's altar."

The cabin door swung open and the trapper entered. The three men immediately asked why he had wired his stove to the rafters.

"Simple," he said. "I had lots of wire and not much stove pipe."

It's easy to miss the obvious when you look at the market only from your perspective.

Market perception is obvious

The market's perception is the obvious one. It might not be what you would like it to be. And you may believe that it's inaccurate or an unfair reflection of your operation. But, true or not, the market's perception of your operation is the reality with which you must deal.

Remember when I said that I believe dairy products are better and fresher at the dairy store than at the jumbo supermarket? It doesn't matter whether the products actually are fresher. That's my perception and, as far as I'm concerned, my perception is reality. If the stores are to market their wares to me, that's the reality they face.

So it is with your customers, suppliers and competitors. Their perception is the reality, as we'll discuss in the next chapter.

What Will Them Dogs Eat?

A dog food company's sales were slipping so the sales manager brought his representatives in for a motivational rally. When the salespeople were all assembled, the sales manager called out to the group:

"What dog food is the most nutritious?"

"Ours!" shouted the group.

"Who has the best advertising campaign?"

"We do!" was the answer.

"And who has the best sales force?"

"We do!" was again the reply.

"Then answer me one question," said the sales manager.

"If our dog food is the most nutritious and if we've got the best advertising campaign and the greatest sales force, then WHY AREN'T WE SELLING MORE DOG FOOD?"

A voice from the back of the room answered,

"'Cause them dogs won't eat it!"

Find out what "them dogs" will eat

We often fail to find out what "them dogs" will eat, or what "them dogs" believe. We confuse our own perception with the market's.

We forget that it's the market's perception that is the reality, not our own.

Not only is the market's perception the reality, it's almost impossible to change that perception once it's established. The market has neither the time nor the interest to investigate the subtle differences between our enterprise and that of our competitor.

The toothpaste test

Stop for a moment and write down the name of the toothpaste you use. Got it? Good, now name four other brands.

If you're like most people, you'll have difficulty coming up with four more brands without a lot of thought. You'll have difficulty because when you decided what brand to use you no longer needed additional information about toothpaste. Your mind stopped accepting information on that subject. If you chose Crest, which most people do, then Aim, Close-Up and Gleem can all spend millions of dollars attempting to get their messages into your head and it will be to no avail.

Customer has a mind filter

The same communication rules apply to you and your business. Once your consumer has made a decision about the marketplace in which you operate, her mind filter ignores additional information about that subject. To penetrate that filter, you must find out what her current perception is and get in step with it rather than try to change it.

Sometimes we get so busy developing and improving our product or service internally that we forget that the marketplace is where the action takes place. We think we know what the market wants or understands so we forget to ask it.

Pringles potato chips

Procter & Gamble failed to ask the market what it wanted before it developed Pringles Potato Chips. In the late 1950s P&G decided to control the potato chip market. Potato chips were traditionally a regional product. P&G decided to corner the market through national distribution. P&G invented a potato chip that could be shipped great distances without breakage and therefore could be distributed nationally. The potato chip could also be stored for long periods without spoilage. P&G created Pringles, the potato chip for the ages.

Then P&G ran television commercials announcing this potato chip breakthrough. These commercials emphasized Pringles' uniform shape and texture. Pringles commercials pointed out that the new potato chip was not easily broken nor was it greasy. Pringles were stacked in a red can and, unlike other potato chips, had no brown spots. Plus Pringles were made in an exciting new way. Proud of itself, P&G charged a ten percent premium for Pringles, the new leading-edge potato chip.

The market didn't buy it. Consumers took one look and decided they didn't want what they perceived to be an artificial potato chip at a ten percent premium. The market didn't care that Pringles could be shipped long distances or that they lasted eighteen months or came stacked in a red can. Consumer's decided Pringles was a false potato chip with a strange taste.

Borden's Wise Potato Chip brand helped the consumer come to this conclusion. Borden's television commercials listed the ingredients in both the Wise and Pringles brands. The announcer read the ingredients off the label.

"In Wise," the announcer said, "you find potatoes. Vegetable oil. Salt.

"In Pringles, you find dehydrated potatoes. Mono- and di-glycerides. Ascorbic acid. Butylated hydroxy-anisole.

"Which do you want to buy?"

Pringles' market share dropped to ten percent, far below expectations. Insiders called it the "Edsel" in P&G's line of products. A somewhat wiser P&G realized they were not bulletproof. Wisely, P&G chose to accept what the market was telling them.

P&G refocused. They improved Pringles, making it a superior potato chip with a different taste and texture. And P&G then sold it at competitive prices instead of at a premium. Today, Pringles has nine new flavors and textures. The potato chip is highly profitable and P&G has trouble satisfying the demand. P&G found out what "them dogs" would eat and gave it to them.

Coca-Cola's New Coke experience

Finding out what "them dogs" will eat is harder than it seems. As we saw in Chapter 4, Coca-Cola learned that when they introduced New Coke in April 1985. Extensive tests had indicated that consumers would prefer the taste of New Coke over both Pepsi Cola and original Coke. So, on the 99th anniversary of the date the first Coca-Cola was sold, the new formula was unveiled with all the hype and advertising you would expect from the world's leading soft drink company.

"Them dogs" didn't like New Coke. Clubs were formed, petitions signed, laws passed, all in support of the original Coke formula. Over 400,000 letters and phone calls of protest were received in Coca-Cola's Atlanta office alone. Two months later, Coca-Cola apologized to the public and brought back the original formula as Classic Coke.

Classic Coke remains the number one soft drink. New Coke, which taste tests still show consumers prefer over Pepsi Cola and Classic Coke, is in tenth place and falling.

Statistics are only one tool

Statistics and blind taste tests may be important but reliance on statistics alone can lead to disaster. You should balance statistics with the subjective analysis your experiences bring to the medicine-pouch process.

"The consumer is sovereign," said Donald Keough, president of Coca-Cola. "We sometimes forget that. In a big company, we tend to be insular and think that we control the market. We don't.

The consumer does. In this case the consumers demanded something from a big company and they got it."

Avon and Tiffany's

Still another big company, Avon, learned the hard way that market perception is reality and that the consumer is sovereign. Avon also learned that market perception is virtually impossible to change.

Avon almost destroyed Tiffany & Co. in the process. Tiffany's was well positioned as a high-service, high-price jewelry store. The name "Tiffany's" had come to mean luxury and exclusivity to millions of shoppers in this country and abroad.

Avon purchased Tiffany's in 1979. Avon depends on rapid inventory turnover rates to be a successful cosmetics mass merchandiser. To achieve these rates, Avon invests fewer dollars in more items and expects faster turnover than was traditional at Tiffany's.

Avon ignored Tiffany's existing market position. Instead, Avon tried to make Tiffany's fit the Avon marketing philosophy. Avon stocked the store with cheap glassware and crystal.

The market was confused. Consumers couldn't understand why this luxurious jewelry store was now featuring $7 wine glasses. A confused consumer doesn't buy, so sales plummeted. In 1984, the last year Avon owned Tiffany's, the store lost $5 million.

So Avon sold Tiffany's to its management. The new owners immediately refocused on Tiffany's luxury jewelry position. Tiffany's own workshop quickly created a $10 million collection of twenty-two individual diamond jewelry pieces. This exotic assemblage of Tiffany's fine craftsmanship was promoted as the "Tiffany Classic Diamond Collection." The collection featured one necklace valued at more than $1 million.

The market was no longer confused. The consumers' perception and Tiffany's operation were once again in tune. Tiffany quit losing money. In fiscal year 1989, Tiffany & Co. earned $24 million on sales of $285 million.

Stay in touch with the market

Market perception is reality and the successful enterprise stays in harmony with it. When company and personal egos ignore this truth, peculiar thinking results.

Company leaders may decide, like those at P&G, Coca-Cola and Avon, that the company is indispensable to the market and therefore controls it.

Such reasoning leads company executives to believe that the sun won't rise in the morning if they don't help it, the world may be a merry-go-round but it'll stop if they aren't pushing it. This logic fails to accept that the world can survive without any single company or person.

Stop and think what Abraham Lincoln, Madame Curie, Mark Twain and Winston Churchill have in common.

They're all dead.

And the world went on anyway. So just how indispensable is any one person or company? If the room in which you're sitting suddenly vanished from the face of the earth with you in it, what would change? There would be holes in the lives with which you are intertwined, but otherwise life would go on much the same.

Some people find that to be a disquieting thought. It isn't really, because accepting the fact that you are dispensable frees you to make the unique contribution only you can make. You no longer have to worry about how the world will survive without you. It'll get along quite nicely. So you don't have to do it all. Instead, you can focus on how you can fit into the world and make your contribution. You're free to discover, accept, develop and capitalize on your unique crackerjack position.

Avis gets in step with the market

Avis Rent-A-Car showed us how recognizing what "them dogs" believe, and then getting in step with that belief, can turn a company around. Avis was struggling as the number two car rental company. Everyone who rented cars on a regular basis knew that

Hertz was the leader. With that perception firmly in mind, consumers made no effort to learn any more about rental cars. Avis spent millions of dollars attempting to get their message into their prospect's head with little progress.

Then Avis recognized that they needed to work with what was already in their prospect's mind, to start with the reality of the marketplace perception. So Avis took a bold step. They admitted that they were number two. This came as no surprise to the consumer. She already knew that. Then Avis related its message to the reality of that marketplace perception. Avis told the consumer what this number-two position meant to her.

Avis capitalizes on number two position

"Because we're number two," Avis said, "we try harder. Because we try harder, you'll find shorter lines, cleaner cars and better service."

The results were spectacular. For thirteen years in a row, Avis had lost money. The first year of the "We try harder" campaign, Avis made $1.2 million. The second year, $2.6 million. The third year, $5 million. Then the company was sold to ITT.

When you accept the reality of how you're perceived in the marketplace, you can work with that perception and establish a position. If you don't honor the consumer's perception, you may deliver mixed messages to your prospect that he either does not hear or will not believe.

Miss America pageant

Look at the Miss America contest. The Miss America organization wants you to consider this event a scholarship pageant rather than a beauty contest, and there is considerable data to support this request. Each year several million dollars in scholarships are offered contestants by the hundreds of state and local pageants, which lead to the ultimate selection of the new Miss America.

One such contest selects Miss Oklahoma. The Kiwanis Club of

Tulsa sponsors the Miss Oklahoma pageant. As a member of the Kiwanis Club, I've worked with the Miss Oklahoma pageant for several years. My jobs have been varied. I've ushered people to their seats, kept overly enthusiastic hair designers away from the contestants, and mixed drinks in the hospitality suite. It wasn't until I became a member of the stage crew, however, that I understood what an opportunity the pageant provides for young women.

The Miss Oklahoma pageant is consistently at or near the top of the Miss America state pageant list in terms of total scholarship money offered to pageant participants. It's possible for a young woman to finance an education by simply competing in the state contest. She doesn't have to win. For example, if she's the only girl to select a particular scholarship offering as her first choice, she gets it regardless of her final ranking.

A contestant who finishes in the top ten is eligible for a substantial scholarship even if she doesn't win the title. A contestant one year came from a family on welfare. At the age of fourteen she told her social worker to quit giving the family money for her particular needs because she'd take care of herself. She went to work as a grocery store sacker and later became a pageant contestant. She finished in the top ten, winning a cash grant and a tuition scholarship, which enabled her to attend and graduate from Oklahoma University. She's now a corporate executive with an annual salary approaching $100,000. Pageant history abounds with such stories.

Market perception ignores scholarships

It's a fact that the Miss America organization gives away millions of dollars in scholarship money. It's also a fact that the scoring system is continually modified to give greater weight to intelligence and talent factors. The market ignores these facts. As long as the pageant administration parades fifty attractive young women across a stage on national television in swimsuits, and as long as they give an award each preliminary night to the outstanding swimsuit participant, the audience will perceive the event to be a beauty contest. The public believes: "If it walks like a duck, looks like a duck and talks like a duck . . . it's a duck."

If the pageant is to get its message across to the general public, it must recognize the reality of the market's perception and get in harmony with that perception. The pageant can learn from Avis and honor what the audience already believes. It can admit that these contestants are among the most beautiful young women in America. Nobody believes the pageant goes looking in closets for homely girls with high IQs or piano talent, so why pretend otherwise?

Thus a strong pageant strategy would be to agree with what the audience already believes, that these fifty contestants are among the most beautiful young women in America. The pageant could say, "In ADDITION to being beautiful, tonight's contestants are intelligent and talented. The Miss America Pageant will award umpteen thousand dollars in scholarships to our bright, talented, and beautiful contestants." The pageant's message would then be in tune with the public perception. Consumers would accept the pageant's stand that factors in addition to beauty have become the major considerations in selecting a winner.

As Coca-Cola president Donald Keough said, "The consumer is sovereign."

If you are to establish a crackerjack position, you must recognize that sovereignty and work with it, not against it.

Check
The
Climate

Plants won't grow in an unfavorable climate. Neither will a business. You have to adjust to the conditions you find like the lady seeking plants for her back yard. "What do you suggest," she asked the nurseryman, "for a spot that gets lots of sun, little rain, has a clay soil and is full of rocks?" He answered, "A sun dial."

If the conditions are not favorable or you don't adjust to meet the conditions then your enterprise will fail. You wouldn't go out on a cold winter morning without checking the weather, would you? The weather can be cruel when you are not prepared. So can the marketplace. Besides, like the plant lady, you might find opportunities you hadn't considered.

Respect the conditions

Sailors check the forecast before going out in a boat. I'm not a sailor, but I am a pilot. I learned how to fly in an Aeronca with no radio or electronic navigation equipment. I soon learned a minor error in calculating wind direction could make a significant difference in where you would arrive. Consequently, you had to keep checking the forecast so you could anticipate any changes in the wind or the weather.

Later, when I was in Air Force flight school, I saw what can happen when you fail to respect the weather. Our class was taken to the flight line one day to look at a huge B-36 airplane that had flown through a thunderstorm. This plane was built to absorb a tremendous beating yet it had barely made it through the hail and wind shears of the thunderstorm. The plane was covered with dimples from the hail. It looked as if an army of elves with ball peen hammers had spent the day beating on the plane.

The message was clear. Go around, over, or under a thunderstorm . . . never through one. Most planes would not have survived the thunderstorm that damaged the B-36. A business that ignores the weather forecast and changing conditions can end up with more than dimples, it can end up on the side of a mountain.

So check the climate. There's no handy weather bureau to give you the market forecast. It's just as well. You'll want to arrive at your own synthesis after checking a variety of sources to see what fits your situation.

Market forecasts are inconsistent

Like weather forecasts, market forecasts are inconsistent. For example, three books published in 1990 dealing with the future disagree with each other on several points.

The books are *Megatrends 2000*, written by John Naisbitt and Patricia Aburdene and published by William Morrow; *Futurescope*, written by Joe Cappo, published by Longman; and *American Renaissance*, written by Marvin Cetron and Owen Davies, published by St. Martin's Press.

The authors agree that America is aging, the educational system is not working, drugs are a crisis and the environment needs saving. They also agree that American values are shifting from self-denial to self-interest and that women will achieve greater status in the 1990s.

However, the authors disagree in other areas. An economic boom is predicted by *Megatrends 2000* and *American Renaissance*, whereas *Futurescope* says that our standard of living will continue to decline. *Futurescope* states that our middle class is shrinking, yet *American Renaissance* believes it's growing.

Apply your own knowledge

Disagreement among experts does not mean you can't use these sources. It means that you must apply your own knowledge and common sense to their conclusions. You'll have to decide how what they say fits your industry, geographical area and operation.

You can see how trends affect us if you will read *Megatrends,* also by John Naisbitt. This book was published in 1982, and it's available in paperback from Warner Books. You can probably find a copy at any bookstore selling used books.

I am suggesting that you read a book published in 1982 because you now have the advantage of looking at Naisbitt's work with the benefit of hindsight. You can see how the broad trends Naisbitt predicted influenced your life in the 1980s. Hindsight will show you that there was nothing very dramatic in the predictions. They were an extrapolation of what you and I can observe on a daily basis if we will but look and then think about what we've seen. That's what Naisbitt did to write *Megatrends* and *Megatrends 2000.* He and his staff determined what the trends were by checking what was covered in the press and how much space was devoted to it. They looked at what was going on around them and then predicted what was going to happen.

The process

Your process is to start with what you know. Then survey the sources closer to your business, and finally consider what the experts say and how broad trends might affect you. Check for any inconsistencies, find out why those exist and what they mean, then create your own weather report.

Nobody can complete this work but you. Books and experts can give you information, and an outside objective consultant can help you direct your thinking. But the final conclusion must be yours because you've got to live with it.

Start with what you already know

When you start with what you already know about the situation, you have a distinct advantage over the experts because you are closer to reality.

Industry experts live in the same cities. They all read the same material, talk to the same sources and then come to the same conclusions. The average person, on the other hand, is in the actual marketplace every day and has a better chance to observe what's really happening.

For example, you can do a substantial amount of meaningful research in the automotive industry by simply looking around a mall or supermarket parking lot. When you see a new car, ask the owner why she bought it. The new owner is proud of her purchase so she'll tell you. It's that simple.

Mrs. Fields cookies

Debbie Fields perfected her recipe for chocolate chip cookies by the time she was seventeen. Over the next few years Debbie watched her husband's business clients, her friends, and her family devour her cookies when they were fresh out of the oven. But when she asked experts if opening a store featuring her unique cookies was a good idea, they answered, "Debbie, nobody will buy your cookies. They're too soft. America loves crispy cookies."

Debbie's personal research said otherwise. She had seen that people didn't want to wait for her cookies to get hard, they wanted them right out of the oven. So Debbie listened to her own research and opened her first store in Palo Alto, California. Now Mrs. Fields Cookies are sold internationally.

You know more than the experts

Peter Lynch, in his book *One Up On Wall Street,* suggests that the average person is in a better position to invest intelligently in the stock market than the experts because the average person is in the marketplace daily. Lynch knows about investing. He managed the $9 billion Fidelity Magellan mutual fund. The Fidelity's fourteen hundred stocks make it the nation's largest mutual fund and its long-term performance is among the best on record.

L'eggs pantyhose

Lynch's wife proved his point. She discovered L'eggs pantyhose in a supermarket. She was pleased with the quality of L'eggs, but she was even more impressed with the concept of buying pantyhose in the supermarket.

Lynch listened to his wife, investigated Hanes, maker of L'eggs, and bought the stock. Lynch's Hanes stock increased six times in value before Hanes was absorbed by Sara Lee.

The L'eggs opportunity sprang from common knowledge available to anybody. Expert analysis of complex reports wasn't required. An open mind receptive to new concepts was. You had to notice the L'eggs racks in thousands of supermarkets or observe women bringing the product home or talk with a supermarket clerk who was selling L'eggs. Once you observed what was happening, it wasn't difficult to see that Hanes might be an investment opportunity.

Helpful publications

You can find a wealth of information in the standard business-oriented periodicals, including *Fortune, Forbes, Business Week, Success,* and *Inc.* The news weeklies, such as *Time, Newsweek* and *U.S. News and World Report,* give you a general overview. You can keep up with social concerns by reading *People* and *USA Today.*

I also read *Advertising Age* because it stays on top of marketing developments. *Sales and Marketing Management* is a respected magazine although I find it too directed to salespeople for my own use. The *Wall Street Journal* deserves its excellent reputation and has been particularly valuable to me since it added its section on marketing.

American Demographics is a monthly publication of Dow Jones & Company that reports on consumer trends for business leaders. A recent edition had articles on how advancing age changes the leisure choices of Americans and a study showing why a few middle-class families became affluent while many more slipped into poverty in the 1980s. The article included forecasts for the 1990s. Not only does the magazine carry helpful articles, it also has advertisements for other research sources.

Several years ago *Mad* magazine was recommended to me because its parodies reflect what is going on in society and are generally well ahead of some of our more traditional sources. I began subscribing and agree with that perception. Besides, its fun. So add it to your list.

The World Future Society

The World Future Society is an association of people interested in how social and technological developments are shaping the future. The Society strives to serve as a neutral clearinghouse for ideas about the future. Ideas about the future include forecasts, recommendations and alternative scenarios. The Society is open to anyone who is interested. Dues are modest.

The Society has an extensive resource catalog with hundreds of books, tapes and other materials dealing with the future. The World Future Society also publishes a number of periodicals. *The Futurist* is a journal of forecasts, trends and ideas about the future. *Futures Research Quarterly* publishes scholarly or technical articles dealing with futures research. *Futures Survey* is a monthly summary of books and articles dealing with future in a broad sense.

For current information, you can contact the World Future Society at 4916 St. Elmo Avenue, Bethesda, Maryland 20814 .

Professional associations as sources

Still another excellent source are the professional associations involved in the industry or industries you are investigating. Associations publish newsletters that discuss the trends in the industry or profession. The newsletters will also deal with questions and problems of interest to association members.

In addition, associations continually study their industry. They run surveys, ask questions and interpret how what's happening on the national scene may affect their members.

One of my clients is a printer. When I talked with the Printing Industry Association, I found more demographic information on the makeup of the printing industry than I could possibly use. The data covered national, regional, state and local statistics and market trends.

Several of my client's customers came from nonprofit and educational institutions. One of the PIA surveys indicated these two specialties to be very large users of printed material. So as we developed a positioning strategy, it made sense to focus on an area that represented a strength of the client as well as a market opportunity that could be exploited.

Association information is generally available to anybody with a serious interest, so explore what's available.

At the public library you can look in the *Gale Encyclopedia of Associations* published by Gale Research Inc. for relevant groups that can send you newsletters, membership directories and information. The Encyclopedia lists more than 20,000 associations and includes addresses and phone numbers.

Gale Research Inc. also publishes the *Gale Directory of Publications and Broadcast Media*. In that book you can find listings for newspapers and magazines that cover your specific area of interest.

Use your library

If you live in a metropolitan area and haven't been to your public library lately, you're in for a pleasant surprise. It's absolutely amazing the wealth of information available through libraries.

The Business and Technology Department of a metropolitan library has information available on all aspects of marketing for a business. You will find all of the periodicals and research reports you'll need, and there will be somebody there delighted to help you find your way through the morass of information available.

Some libraries provide a fee-based library service that will do research for you. The fees are on a time-used basis and are modest compared with an independent research firm.

Through such a service, a library professional will search library materials, make copies and contact experts and other outside sources for information. They will do this on a confidential basis for your exclusive use.

A typical service has over a thousand on-line databases to provide research. They can find a list of articles on the latest trends in a particular industry as well as information on new products or services being developed that may compete with yours.

If you have a computer with a modem, you can take advantage of a free dial-up access service offered by some libraries. This service will connect you to the library's computerized catalog and community information files.

Libraries talk to each other and share resources, so if your library hasn't got it, they can get it.

Not only that, it's been my experience that you simply won't find more helpful people than you find at the library. They are excited about all they can do and welcome the opportunity to do it. So by all means, go to the library.

Potential sources of business research

The local, state and national chambers of commerce can provide economic information. Even the smallest chamber will have basic demographics for its market.

Newspapers analyze their markets. Regional and national advertisers want to know what to expect, and newspapers provide them with that information. Most newspapers are very cooperative in giving their research publications to anyone with an interest.

Information services

If you have a computer with a modem and the appropriate communications software you can get a wealth of information from electronic information libraries. There are hundreds of services available.

Pricing methods vary from service to service. Some charge an origination fee plus a flat monthly charge. Others charge by actual usage. Prices may vary depending on time of day and so forth. There are many variations and combinations of fee structures.

The Dow Jones News Retrieval (DJNR) service is an example of a serious business research source. As of this writing it consists of 46 databases, most of them aimed at users who want abundant information in a hurry. It includes current, real-time and historical stock quotes, the latest information from such sources as the *Washington Post,* the *Wall Street Journal, Barron's,* and the Dow Jones News Service. It also provides "Wall Street Week" transcripts, a professional investor report, and general services including movie and book reviews.

The DJNR fees vary depending on time of day. Non-prime time-after 6 p.m. is approximately 10 percent of prime time fees. The service provides an inexpensive starter kit including three free hours of search time in the first 30 days.

New electronic information services come into being every day. Check with your library to see what current offerings are available.

Formal research is not the complete answer

Frequently we lack the faith to believe in our own gut feeling about a situation so we look to a research firm for the answer. We want to rely on a scientific survey or poll rather than our own analysis. We believe the poll will give us the absolute truth because a research firm did it.

Research firms tell us not to do that. They tell us that research is only a tool and that we should use it as a tool in coming to our own conclusions. Standing alone, a poll does not provide the answer. And the poll itself should be examined closely.

Investigate poll methodology

There are several questions you should ask when looking at poll results. To be accurate a survey should be taken from a random sampling of at least 400 respondents. So investigate the number of respondents. You should also learn how they were selected.

The accuracy of polls is being further weakened by the increasing refusal of Americans to participate. In 1990 thirty-six percent of consumers refused to answer a question over the phone. This is a twelve percent increase over 1986, according to Walker Research. Yet many polling companies still rely heavily on phone interviews.

It's important to know when a poll was taken because it's only an estimate of an opinion at that particular time. It's like a snapshot. It gives you the picture at that exact moment. Subsequent activities could change the results significantly.

Be sure you know who conducted the poll, for whom it was done, and any potential conflict of interest.

Be skeptical of mail-back or phone-in polls. Read the survey questions carefully for fairness and clarity.

Again, the most important caveat is that you judge poll results in conjunction with other knowledge you have about the situation and don't let it become the total answer. A poll is only one factor in the equation.

Collecting information is not the problem

You can quickly be buried in data. So be selective. Don't try to read all of these books, publications, reports, polls, etc. If you do, you'll find yourself in a thunderstorm while you're still trying to confirm that it might rain. As you assimilate information, you'll begin to sense opportunities. You'll want to test these opportunities to make sure they are valid. One of the questions you'll want answered is whether your potential opportunity springs from a trend or a fad. And we'll look at that next.

A Fad
Or A
Trend?

When I was in the shopping center business, I learned about fads and trends. Most of the time, leasing retail space in a shopping center was hard work. You made cold sales calls, followed up leads and negotiated leases with sophisticated tenants.

That all changed when a fad came along. Fads made the phone ring. Everybody wanted to rent shopping center space for video game arcades. Video games were quickly installed everywhere so there was no need for arcades. Later it was tanning salons. Concerns about the effects of tanning the skin squelched interest in tanning salons.

When lots of folks want to rush into a business they know nothing about, you can bet it's a fad.

Suburban shopping centers are the result of a trend. As families became mobile, they migrated to the suburbs. Recognizing this trend, developers built shopping centers to serve the populace. More people meant larger centers with better shopping choices. People no longer went downtown to shop so major retail stores closed. From time to time efforts are made to revitalize downtown shopping. These attempts seldom work because they are in direct conflict with the continuing migration to the suburbs. People will not go downtown to shop unless there is a reason, and there is no reason.

It's important to differentiate between fads and trends when you're filling your medicine pouch with information.

What's a "fad"?

A fad generally comes racing onto the scene. Everybody is talking about it. It's on television. It's in the newspapers. Quickie books are written about it. New magazines cover the action. And almost as quickly the fad vanishes.

It's like a skyrocket on the Fourth of July. Much action. Much attraction. Then, whoosh, it's gone. We're attracted to fads for the same reasons we like skyrockets. They're beautiful, burn with intense heat, attract everybody's attention and are fun. Fads are exciting and invigorating. There's no reason not to chase a fad or two as long as you know what you're doing. But don't depend on a fad for your livelihood or you may end up like a spent skyrocket.

Fads are like lightning. And, like lightning, they seldom hit the same place twice. The only company that has been able to create more than one fad is Wham-O. Wham-O had huge successes with the Hula Hoop, Frisbee and Superball. But even Wham-O has not had a runaway success in the past 20 years.

Rubik's Cube

Rubik's Cube exemplifies a typical fad. The Cube was developed by an obscure Hungarian architectural professor who earned less than $200 a week. Rubik had no desire to start a business. He had developed his Cube as a visual aid for his classes.

The Cube had all the attributes of a successful fad. It came from a humble beginning and quickly captured the public's imagination. The Cube was addictive because the premise was seductively simple. All you had to do was scramble the colored panels and then put them back together again. Most people couldn't do it but kept coming back anyway because they refused to believe they could be defeated by a multicolored plastic cube.

Rubik sold over 100 million Cubes in two short years. Competitors leaped into the market. The public soon became bored and the skyrocket ran out of fuel.

Rubik tried to duplicate his fad with Rubik's Magic. Rubik's Magic is a flat strip of plastic panels bound by thick elastic bands. The challenge is to flip the panels out of place and then try to put them back in order. Rubik's Magic didn't make it in spite of worldwide distribution through Matchbox International. The puzzle was too abstract.

Cabbage Patch dolls

Perhaps the greatest fad craze of all time occurred in 1983 with the Cabbage Patch dolls created by Xavier Roberts. Roberts was fascinated by all forms of art. In 1976, when he was not yet 21, Roberts happened upon an old dog-eared library book about an early nineteenth-century German folk art called "needle molding." Today the craft is known as "soft sculpture." He mastered the art and soon began turning out soft sculpture dolls, each with its own unique expression.

Roberts called them "Little People," and when asked about them said they were found "in the cabbage patch." Roberts didn't intend to sell the dolls, so when he was first asked to sell one, he said that the dolls weren't for sale but perhaps they could be adopted.

An ugly little doll with its own name and individual expression that could not be bought but must be adopted was a unique toy concept. The concept was slow to catch on but gathered momentum as the word spread. "Adoptions" soon outstripped Roberts's ability to meet demand. Roberts sold the rights to make "Cabbage Patch Kids" to the Coleco Toy Company.

Coleco was the fifth-largest toy maker in America but even they couldn't manufacture enough dolls to handle the demand as Cabbage Patch doll madness swept America in the fall of 1983.

Women's magazines touted the Kids as an excellent Christmas present. "Today" hostess Jane Pauley, pregnant at the time, received one as a gift and gave it 5-1/2 minutes on the show. *Time*, *Fortune* and the *Wall Street Journal* wrote about the Kids. Bob Hope featured the Cabbage Patch Kids in a ten-minute sketch on his Christmas TV special.

Stores were hopelessly understocked. Coleco made heroic efforts to satisfy the craze, including airlifting the Kids from Hong Kong via 747s. Demand was high. Supplies were low. Riots ensued. In Charleston, West Virginia, five thousand shoppers stormed Hill's Department Store seeking one of only 120 Kids in stock. The scene was repeated across the country.

A single edition of the *Washington Post* carried forty-eight classified ads for the dolls, with asking prices as low as $30 for a Cabbage Patch Kid to $3,000 for a Little Person, Roberts's handcrafted version. Cartier in Beverly Hills asked the top price for a Cabbage Patch Kid. The Kid's name was Aretha Flori. She came with a sapphire necklace, a diamond bracelet, and diamond earrings. The adoption fee was $35,000.

The Cabbage Patch Kids phenomena continued through 1985. Sales were approximately $60 million in 1983, over $500 million in 1984, and peaked at $600 million in 1985. Sales fell in 1986 to $200 million and continued to decline to slightly over $100 million in 1987.

The Cabbage Patch Kid skyrocket stayed aloft longer than most. The result ultimately was the same. Like a hot-air balloon, Coleco soared high on Cabbage Patch Kid sales. When those sales fell, down came Coleco.

Coleco scrambled to diversify. Its Adam home computer was full of glitches and failed. Trivial Pursuit was hot, but Coleco paid a high price for the game just as its popularity peaked. Coleco filed for bankruptcy. In 1989 Hasbro acquired the company's remaining assets and Coleco went out of business. The Cabbage Patch Kid line is now an established part of Hasbro. Sales of

Cabbage Patch Kid dolls and accessories are good but nothing close to sales in the mid '80s.

Urban cowboy

When you see an exciting new development being reported with great intensity and excitement, there's a good chance you're dealing with a fad. Beware or you can become another Gilley's.

Remember the "urban cowboy" craze? It began in the late 1970s and peaked in 1980, when the movie *Urban Cowboy* starring John Travolta was released. The movie featured a Houston night club called Gilley's.

Gilley's grew from a honky-tonk with a capacity of five hundred to a huge hall, where almost five thousand people could crowd in to hear people like Willie Nelson sing. Gilley's was exciting. It had lots of side shows in addition to country music. There were forty pool tables. For fifty cents you could hit a punching bag and show off your strength. If you hit it hard enough, a siren went off. Gilley's feature attraction was a mechanical bucking bull used to train rodeo riders. For two dollars you could try to stay on board. Many Gilley's patrons became expert mechanical bull riders.

Practically overnight, being "country" became "cool." Country music bars sprang up on every corner. Huge establishments with names like "Billy Bob's" or "Duke's" or "Willie's" became the fashion, and there was a run on mechanical bulls.

Folks danced the cotton-eyed Joe, drank beer from long-neck bottles, smoked Marlboro cigarettes and dipped snuff. Patrons wore cowboy hats, leather belts with their names carved on the backs, boots and Levi's bluejeans. Willie Nelson entertained at the White House and was on the cover of *Life* and *Newsweek*. Country music radio stations popped up all over the dial. Barbara Mandrell had a hit television variety show.

About 1983 the craze began to fade. Across the country, bars took down saddles, sold their mechanical bulls and hung up old washboards and Coca-Cola signs. Barbara Mandrell retired to Nashville, bluejeans sales plummeted, and Ronald Reagan did not invite Willie Nelson to the White House. As country music went out of fashion so did Gilly's. Entertainer Mickey Gilley owned a small part of the club that carried his name, and he complained to principal owner Sherwood Cryer about the deterioration. Court battles ensued, and in 1988 Gilley won a $17 million judgment against Cryer. Cryer filed bankruptcy and in March 1989 Gilley's closed its doors.

Country music is enjoying new popularity in the 1990s. This time it appears the music is the driving force and not urban cowboy glitter. Either way it's too late for operations like Gilley's whose survival was dependent on the support of trend-chasing fans.

Building a business on fads is not impossible but it requires an extraordinary sense of timing. The people who ran Coleco were very knowledgeable toy merchants whose timing was off. Coleco relied on Cabbage Patch Kids too long and purchased additional toy lines such as Trivial Pursuit at just the wrong time.

Franklin Computer

Franklin Computer of Pennsauken, New Jersey, is a company that has successfully functioned in fad markets. Franklin operates in a market where today's novelty is next year's commodity. In that market, Franklin has carved out a niche with electronic spellers and dictionaries.

As each new technology is developed, Franklin markets an expensive machine incorporating that technology through Sharper Image and other high-toned distributors. As competitors invariably catch up to the new technology, Franklin marks its leading edge model down and broadens the model's distribution. Then Franklin introduces a new model with still newer technology at the top of the market.

Franklin has had as many as twenty electronic spellers and dictionaries on the market at the same time, each with its own target market.

Franklin's strategy generates massive free advertising at the top, together with an aura of status and quality. As Franklin then brings the product down in stages, it makes high profit margins at each level. Such merchandising requires a sensitive feel for the market and is not for the fainthearted.

Fads are unpredictable

Fads are virtually impossible to predict. One expert, Chaytor Mason, who is a psychologist and professor at the University of Southern California, says, "A fad begins when we discover that there's a facet of our personality which has previously been unexpressed or inexpressible. The fad provides the means, or the excuse, to satisfy that facet." Examples include message T-shirts, vanity license plates and bumper stickers.

There is simply no way of knowing what will become a fad. No conventional market research could have predicted that millions of people would buy plastic tubes to swing around their hips and call them "Hula Hoops."

Position with trends, not fads

If you like living on the edge, try sky diving. In business you'll be better off looking at the trends instead. A trend sneaks up on us. It's like a glacier. Everybody can see it and everybody knows it's moving, but few people pay any attention. A trend doesn't have the fascinating attraction of a fad so it's overlooked. It doesn't get the media spotlight. It's just there, quietly getting stronger every day.

We know our population is aging. We know people are leaving rural areas and moving to the city. We know the consumption of cigarettes and alcohol is declining. We know all these trends and tend to discount them because they are not flashy. Yet it's foolish to ignore them when choosing a crackerjack position, just as it would be foolish to build a home in the path of a glacier and expect that home to remain there forever.

So if what you're considering has all the excitement of a skyrocket, it's probably a fad, which will burn out and may leave you stranded. If it's dull and plodding it's probably a trend, and the wise course is to go the same direction it's going. A trend won't carry your enterprise because it doesn't move fast enough. That's what makes it a trend. But a trend won't leave you stranded either.

Chambers Development Company

John Rangos is one of America's richest entrepreneurs, with a fortune estimated in excess of $400 million. He achieved that lofty position by following a trend that everybody knew about.

"Rangos didn't know anything that wasn't in the papers," said one of his competitors' attorneys. "The only difference is that he did something about it."

Rangos is president and chief executive officer of Chambers Development Co. Chambers Development is in the trash and landfill business.

Use common sense

It's been common knowledge for many years that Americans are throwing away more rubbish each year and that much of that rubbish will never disintegrate. Every expert remotely associated with the trash business has, therefore, consistently predicted that landfills would become extremely valuable, particularly if they met increasingly stringent environmental standards.

Rangos developed a simple plan in line with this widely recognized trend. His plan was to find landfill sites, acquire them, then get collection contracts to use the landfills effectively. He's been doing this since the early 1970s.

Chambers Development now has trash-hauling companies, municipal contracts and landfill space from Rhode Island to Alabama. Industry estimates are that Chambers has enough landfill space to handle their needs well into the next century.

Establishing a position in line with generally accepted trends offers lucrative long-term opportunities. Leave the fads to your competitors and stick with trends.

A Look At Your Market

It's important to know your position in your market. It's also important to know the dynamics of that specific market. For example, just how easy is it for new competitors to enter your market? Some markets are hard to enter, others are simple. A market that is hard to enter is not necessarily better than an easy one, or vice versa. They simply require different strategies.

Government franchise

The government can make a market difficult to enter. Radio and television broadcasting station licenses are examples of the government's power to limit competition.

When I was in the radio station business, it was difficult to enter. There is a finite number of radio frequencies available in a given market and somebody has to make those allocations. That somebody is the Federal Communications Commission. So when the FCC grants you a license, it amounts to a franchise to operate in that specific market.

The growth of FM broadcasting and improved technology created more frequency possibilities, so it's not as difficult to enter the market as it once was. But you still have to have a license to play the game.

Capital-requirement franchise

Capital requirements also limit competition. The newspaper industry is an example. Unlike broadcasting, no licenses are granted to operate a newspaper. There are no franchises. However, starting a daily newspaper requires a major capital investment. You have to hire the staff, buy the equipment to print the newspaper, acquire trucks to deliver the paper, establish a circulation base and so forth, all before the first advertisement can be sold.

It's virtually impossible to start a successful new daily newspaper of any significant size because of the investment required. In major markets, newspapers are not starting. They are merging or going out of business altogether.

You can't start a new *large* daily newspaper, but you can start a *small* one. Technology makes it possible for small, limited-interest newspapers to be published economically. Computer software makes it possible for one person to set the type and lay out the newspaper. Press time can be hired. As a result there has been a proliferation of "shoppers" and neighborhood newspapers focusing on small segments of the large daily newspaper's traditional circulation area. So far the market has room for both small and large newspapers.

Some businesses are easy to enter

Some businesses require no license and very little capital to enter. Public speaking is such a business.

I enjoy public speaking. It's fun, great for my ego, and I get paid for doing it. It's nice to get paid for doing something you enjoy. It's difficult, however, to make a living from speaking by itself. One reason it's difficult is it's easy for competitors to enter the business. All a person has to do is announce "I'm a speaker" and he's a competitor.

Are you easy to replace?

Earl Nightingale said that your compensation will be dependent upon three things:

1. What you do.
2. The ability with which you do it.
3. The difficulty replacing you.

How difficult are you to replace? Are there substitutes available, or are you the only choice?

A generic public speaker, for example, is easily replaced. Being easy to replace is a second reason that it's difficult to make a living in the speaking profession. A program planner can often find an adequate speaker for less money, unless the speaker is positioned as THE expert on the subject the program planner wants to cover. Of course, that's what crackerjack positioning is all about . . . positioning your operation as the only choice when the need for what you do arises.

Buyer controls market

If it's easy for competitors to enter the game and provide the consumer with a choice, and if it's easy for clients or customers to substitute something else for what you do, then it follows that the customer or client has the power to control the market. With so many resources available, buyers can hold prices down and make it difficult to survive.

Landscape maintenance business

The Tulsa, Oklahoma, landscape maintenance business is a case in point. This market's dynamics demonstrate what can happen when it's simple for competitors to enter the game and when it's relatively easy to replace existing players.

A great many people suddenly became unemployed in Tulsa when the oil business took a turn for the worse in the mid-1980s.

Many of these unemployed people decided to mow lawns to survive.

A popular story at the time asked: "How many geologists can you get in a pickup truck?" The answer: "Two . . . and their lawn mowers."

Easy to enter, easy to replace

It was simple to enter the lawn-mowing business. All you needed was a lawn mower. Not much skill or training was required. And it was easy to replace an existing player. There wasn't a lot of product differentiation in lawn mowing.

Overnight, the Tulsa lawn maintenance market was in chaos. With so many sources to choose from, the lawn owner negotiated tough prices, which lead to bloody competition.

Established lawn maintenance companies suddenly found themselves in a war. Those companies were burdened with large investments in mowers, weed eaters, trucks, leaf blowers, etc. They also had relatively high overhead with offices, full-time employees and all the associated expenses.

Increased competition

In normal times those established companies would have contracted for landscape work at a profit. Suddenly, they found themselves in competition with amateurs who bid jobs at a loss either through ignorance or desperation to bring in any cash possible.

Established companies continued to control the larger jobs because the amateurs lacked the equipment and expertise to compete at this level. However, it was the residential and smaller commercial jobs that often made the difference between a profit and a loss, even for the big companies. This work was now fair game. Loss of that work created financial pressures for the established operators.

Ultimately the market stabilized. No matter how desperate you are, you can't operate at a loss indefinitely, so most of the amateurs went away. However, market stabilization came too late for some of the big companies. The oversupply of competitors forced them to merge or go out of business.

This potential for overnight chaos exists in any market that can be easily entered or provides products and services that aren't difficult to replace. You need to be aware of that potential volatility so you can plan accordingly.

Four market stages

In addition to knowing how easy the market is to enter and how simple it is to replace the players, you'll also want to know the status of the market. Markets, like products and services, go through four steps in their life cycles.

1. Start Up
2. Growth
3. Maturity
4. Decline

Health and fitness industry

A current growth market is the health and fitness industry. People are more conscious of what they eat and what they must do to stay healthy. Shoppers now read labels to see what ingredients are in the food they buy. Sales of exercise equipment for the home are growing at a rapid rate. Hospitals have created their own exercise facilities, and teach courses on exercise and nutrition.

Markets perceived to be in conflict with health and fitness are in decline. The domestic cigarette market has reached maturity and is fading. Coffee drinking is also declining. So is the consumption of alcohol.

A market should not be avoided just because it's mature or declining. Low-growth industries have some advantages. Products are not made obsolete overnight, and the competition is not as fierce.

Tobacco companies maintain low profile

In 1991, sales of cigarettes declined for the 10th year in a row. Conventional efforts by tobacco companies to market their wares in this environment such as targeting women and minorities have attracted strong criticism. So the companies are focusing their efforts on the one-third of Americans who still smoke. R.J. Reynolds, Brown & Williamson and Philip Morris are spending millions of dollars to build data bases with the names, addresses, and brand preferences of smokers. They do this with cents-off coupons, premiums such as T-shirt and belt buckle giveaways, and free samples. The companies then target these smokers through direct mail to entice them to switch brands. The companies thereby avoid criticism that they are encouraging people, particularly youngsters, to start smoking.

Brew pubs and micro-breweries

Overall beer consumption is flat. The major brands are slugging it out for a bigger share of the dwindling market. While that battle rages, there is a boomlet in brew pubs and micro-breweries across the country. Brew pubs feature a micro-brewery in a restaurant environment. The pub then brews beer for consumption on the premises. The beers have exotic names and provide a "you can only get it here" panache for the restaurant. Brew pubs are springing up all over the country, thanks to compact beer-making equipment and more permissive laws allowing the brewing of small amounts of beer for on-premises consumption.

Micro-breweries differ from brew pubs in that most of their production is placed in bottles or kegs to be consumed elsewhere. Fritz Maytag is credited with pioneering the micro-brewing industry. Maytag is a descendent of the founder of the giant washer-and-dryer company that bears his name. In 1965 Maytag purchased the Anchor Brewing Co. in San Francisco shortly before the brewery was to be closed. Maytag invested both his inheritance and the next ten years of his life to make the brewery profitable. Now

Anchor sells all the beer it can produce and has a following from coast to coast.

In 1989 there were more than 125 micro-breweries in the country and 65 brew pubs. Both types of breweries are growing at a rapid rate. Even so, the total production of brew pubs and micro-breweries is less than 1/10 of one percent of all beer brewed and sold in the United States. Today's consumers want choices. This demand makes profitable market niches available, even in a declining industry.

Gourmet coffee

The coffee market is no different. Major coffee brands are battling it out for market share in a declining market. The market is declining but consumers are still demanding choices. This demand makes it possible for small coffee growers to carve out narrow but profitable market positions in spite of the shrinking demand.

Kona Coffee from the Big Island of Hawaii has such a market niche. Tourists are discovering the unique taste of Kona Coffee as more and more tourists visit Hawaii. Hawaii is the only place in the United States where coffee is grown commercially. The Arabica variety coffee has thrived in the rich volcanic soil of Kona since its first planting in the early 1800s.

The Captain Cook Coffee Company Ltd. is one company serving this market niche. The company is located in the hamlet of Captain Cook in the heart of the coffee land. The Captain Cook Coffee Company dries, mills and roasts the coffee cherries on location and then sells the finished product to tourists, both on the premises and by mail. Its share of the total coffee market is infinitesimal but still sufficient to support a modest operation with a specialized niche.

Success possible in declining market

A declining market is not necessarily an inhospitable one. Niche marketing opportunities exist. Brew pub and micro-brewery seg-ments of the beer industry illustrate these opportunities. Kona coffee and limited-circulation newspapers are other examples.

The opportunity to locate and serve a narrow slice of a shrink-ing market is found in professions as well as business and industry.

Law firm positions in declining market

One of my clients is a law firm that specializes in the oil-and-gas industry. Most of the major law firms in Tulsa had oil-and-gas departments during the early 1980s oil boom. Competition was fierce but the market was growing so all the firms did well.

Then came the bust.

What had been a strong growth market suddenly went into a steep decline. Many law firms closed their oil-and-gas depart-ments.

My client was concerned about its position in this declining market. The firm was faced with a difficult choice. Should it reposition and seek more exciting growth markets such as envi-ronmental law or hazardous waste? Or should it stay with oil-and-gas work?

Whereas there was no question that the oil-and-gas market was declining, a cross-check of all the market elements showed that my client's market position was definitely not going down with the market.

Firm's position stronger than ever

The firm's competitors had abandoned the oil-and-gas playing field or, at best, maintained a token presence. As a result, my client had become the pre-eminent oil-and-gas law firm by de-fault. Not only had the firm become the leader in the field, it had also acquired a certain cachet as a survivor in this battered indus-try — a firm that had stuck it out with other companies still active in oil and gas.

So the firm's decision was to take an even stronger position in the oil-and-gas industry. The firm began to publicize its faith and expertise in the business. As the firm's position became better known and more strongly entrenched, new clients from outside the firm's natural geographical market turned to my client for oil-and-gas legal work.

It's possible to do well in a declining market if you realize what the market is doing and adjust your strategy accordingly.

Growth markets are exciting

Growth markets seem to be much more exciting than declining ones. And they are. Prospecting for gold is exciting too. But like gold prospecting, if you make a major discovery in a growth market, you can count on attracting a lot of company overnight. The increased competition may force you into growing faster than is wise.

Business history is full of tales about companies operating in fast-growing industries that suddenly disappear. The company flourishes and doubles in size. It doubles again and still again. And then, poof, it vanishes. The company gets so caught up in the growth cycle that it's unprepared for the moment when demand slackens or a better mousetrap appears. The market turns and, like a Pac Man, gobbles up the company.

People Express

People Express was such a company. Donald Burr founded People Express following government deregulation of the airline industry. He capitalized on the newly created growth market by offering no-frills flights at rock-bottom prices. People Express operated profitably on these fares by keeping operating costs low through revolutionary practices such as the hub-and-spoke distribution system now used by virtually all airlines and a staff of nonunion employees who owned stock in the company.

Head-to-head competition doesn't work

People Express's strategy was successful as long as Burr refrained from competing head-to-head with the major carriers. However, Burr became convinced that the major airlines' operating costs were so high they wouldn't cut fares to compete with him, so he began to expand at breakneck speed and went after a share of the majors' most lucrative routes. The majors retaliated by slashing fares, which plummeted the entire industry into heavy losses.

People Express briefly retreated, then plunged into expansion again by purchasing Frontier Airlines and attempting to merge the unionized full-service airline with its nonunion, no-frills operation. The result was a disaster. Frontier's losses quickly drained People Express, and the remaining skeleton operation was absorbed by Texas International. Burr's rapid expansion program in direct competition with established competitors destroyed the airline.

You must be quick on your feet and ever alert to change if you're to survive and prosper in a growth market. Sooner or later the market will change and you must be ready. Nothing lasts forever.

Works in all market cycles

Successful crackerjack positioning is possible in all types of markets, be they start-up, growth, mature or declining. A crackerjack positioning niche can be established in a market open to all competitors, each of whom can easily be replaced. It can also be achieved in a flat or declining market. And it can be secured in a growth market. To achieve such a position requires knowing what's happening, how it's affecting the market, and adjusting your strategy accordingly.

Know The Enemy

"If you know the enemy and know yourself, you need not fear the result of a hundred battles. If you know yourself but not the enemy, for every victory gained you will also suffer a defeat. If you know neither the enemy nor yourself, you will succumb in every battle . . . "

Sun Tzu

Sun Tzu's *The Art of War* was written some 2,500 years ago. His precepts apply to today's world of business as surely as they did to the art of war 2,500 years ago.

"To fight and conquer in all your battles is not supreme excellence," said Sun Tzu. "Supreme excellence consists in breaking the enemy's resistance without fighting."

And so it is with crackerjack positioning. Crackerjack positioning strategy is designed to put you into a position where you own your market niche and it's virtually impossible for anybody to take it away from you as long as you do your job. As Sun Tzu advises, you will have succeeded in "breaking the enemy's resistance without fighting." But first you have to know who the enemy is and what they're doing.

It takes more than hard work

Far too often we believe that if we just work hard, if we just "put our nose to the grindstone and our shoulder to the wheel," if we just practice positive thinking, then we can accomplish anything.

That simply isn't true.

If your competitor already owns the position you want, you cannot have it no matter what you do. Like a parking place that already has a car in it, that position is occupied; and unless your enemy moves or makes a major tactical error, you can't have it.

Custer's last stand

General George Armstrong Custer learned at the Battle of the Little Bighorn that experience and dedication are not enough.

There is still controversy and difference of opinion as to exactly what happened on that battlefield, but there's no disagreement that Custer's fatal mistake was attacking the Sioux Indians alone. Custer had 225 well-trained cavalrymen who were experienced in Indian fighting. Custer believed that he and his men could out-fight any number of Indians regardless of their position.

Custer was mistaken. Some 2,000 Sioux warriors were entrenched in their position and Custer's troop was wiped out. All the experience, confidence, positive thinking, "shoulder to the grindstone," etc., will not enable an outside force to overcome a well entrenched position.

Look at the market

So you look at the market. You have to be willing to give your competitors the positions they already occupy and find your own elsewhere.

This is difficult to do. We believe so strongly that we can overcome any disadvantage that, like Custer, we willingly plunge into battle against fortified competitors. Believe me, you can't win.

IBM, Xerox and RCA

Xerox took on IBM and lost. Xerox spent millions of dollars learning that the market believed "Xerox" meant "copier" and not "computer." Then IBM returned the favor. IBM invested millions of dollars to learn that "IBM" meant "computer" and not "copier."

IBM and Xerox survived. RCA didn't. RCA spent $250 million struggling against IBM and lost. RCA was so preoccupied with fighting the computer war that it also lost its position in radio and television to the Japanese, and it ultimately disappeared.

Changing market provides new niche

One of my clients is a regional supermarket chain. The company is owned locally and is managed by the third generation of the founding family.

For many years the business successfully operated from 25,000-square-foot locations. At one time the company had seven stores.

Then the market changed. Along came 60,000-square-foot warehouse supermarkets. These stores offered a limited but adequate selection of products at rock-bottom prices. To be successful, the jumbo supermarkets must have a large sales volume, but they have the store sizes and prices to attract that volume.

Head-to-head competition doesn't work

Market dynamics had changed. My client simply could not compete head-to-head with these giants. But it tried. It gave up distributing S&H Green Stamps because the cost of the stamps increased the prices my client must charge to be profitable. It added the words "Super Saver" to its name and went to war.

Fortunately the company was debt-free. It had the resources to survive as it was being rebuffed by its new competitors and its sales continued to decline.

But the company could see, figuratively speaking, that the light at the end of the tunnel was from an oncoming train, and if it stayed on this track it would be crushed. That company's head-to-head strategy was not going to work no matter how hard it tried. It didn't matter how positively the company thought. It was out-gunned and therefore doomed.

Look for alternatives

So we went into the marketplace to find alternatives. We learned that people believed that the giant stores offered an adequate variety of satisfactory products at generally lower prices than my client. And their perception was essentially correct.

We also learned that the huge stores could not provide the personal service and warm atmosphere of a smaller store owned and operated by the third generation of a local family. Nor could such a huge store offer customized delivery service at reasonable rates.

Niche marketing strategy works

Reluctantly my client gave up fighting the head-to-head price battle it could not win. I say "reluctantly" because none of us wants to admit defeat of any kind and my client was no different.

The company dropped "Super Saver" from its logo and added "Family Foods . . . serving Tulsa since 1950." My client offered additional services such as money orders, movie tickets, postage stamps, etc. And it began delivering groceries.

One day a customer asked if my client would deliver groceries anyplace in Tulsa. My client replied that it might, depending on the circumstances. What did the customer have in mind?

Quite a bit, it turned out. It seemed that the customer was head of the Tulsa Public School Home Economics Department. The department's teachers had difficulty getting groceries delivered. The department also had a problem getting billing handled in a convenient manner. My client custom-designed a delivery and billing system that fit the department's requirements. The company added a $40-50 thousand per year account and established a position and relationship with a client that would be very difficult to take away.

Market fragmentation provides opportunities

As markets fragment, profitable crackerjack positions become available. There is no need to go head-to-head against a strong competitor. You can choose another course. Markets constantly evolve, and each new evolution generates opportunities.

Look at the hamburger market

McDonald's is far and away the hamburger market leader. McDonald's is as American as apple pie, motherhood and the flag. It's the epitome of success, the crowning example of the American Dream.

McDonald's began with a simple concept. Ray Kroc believed it was possible to nationalize what had been a mom and pop operation, the hamburger stand.

McDonald's offered a cheap hamburger. It built its reputation by creating that hamburger from quality ingredients and delivering it promptly. In the beginning, the hamburgers were all take-out. McDonald's had no room for its customers to sit down. McDonald's wanted you to pick up your burgers and be on your way.

As McDonald's grew and flourished, its stores became larger. Costs increased and people began to stay and eat at McDonald's. Television advertising promoted the experience of eating at McDonald's rather than the food itself. Takeout business was still important so McDonald's added drive-by service windows.

In its first twenty-two years, McDonald's built 4,177 stores in the United States and twenty-one other countries and reached $1 billion in total revenue. It took IBM forty-six years and Xerox sixty-three years to reach that same revenue level. McDonald's was "king of hamburger hill."

Burger King proves you can't go head-to-head

What kind of success would you expect to have, going head-to-head against a market leader like McDonald's? Ask Burger King. Burger King tackled the titan on its own turf and has the scars to prove it.

Between 1976 and 1990, Burger King went through four advertising agencies and eight different campaigns trying to take market share from McDonald's. Some of the early campaigns (notably "Have It Your Way," which ran from 1974 to 1976) were fairly successful. The "Have It Your Way" campaign appealed to the consumer's desire to be treated as an individual. The campaign contrasted Burger King's flexibility with McDonald's cookie-cutter operation. For reasons totally beyond my comprehension, Burger King abandoned this campaign.

Burger King has headed downhill ever since the $40 million "Herb the Nerd" advertising campaign flopped in 1986. Between 1987 and 1990, Burger King's share of the market slipped from 19.9 percent to 19.2 percent, while McDonald's lead widened to 46.5 percent. So much for knocking heads with the market leader.

McDonald's leaves niche market opportunity

While Burger King focuses on a battle with McDonald's, other burger kiosks are popping up on shopping center parking lots across the country, taking advantage of the original cheap hamburger position McDonald's has now abandoned. McDonald's has expanded its menu. In addition to hamburgers, you can have breakfast at McDonald's. You can also have salads and chicken, even pizza at selected locations. Who knows what will come next?

When McDonald's enlarged its stores and expanded its menu, the company left its original basic hamburger position open. The shopping center hamburger kiosk fills this position by serving a simple hamburger and its accouterments through a takeout window.

Each position has room for only one occupant

Today's segmented society has room for many positions, but each position has room for only one occupant. When you know which positions your competitors occupy, you won't waste valuable time and resources trying to fill the same slots. You can then find other positions that will work. If you don't do that, you will not survive.

Bookstore fails to position

One of my saddest experiences in the shopping center business was watching a neighborhood bookstore fail because the proprietor would not position herself by specializing.

One day I dropped in at the store and asked her to step outside with me.

"Margaret," I said, "you've got to specialize if you are to survive. See that grocery store over there next to that variety store? Both those stores carry the same books that you do. They have more traffic, and they sell those books at a *discount*. You've got a strong science fiction customer base. Why not position yourself as THE science fiction bookstore in Tulsa?"

"Because," she said, "I don't like science fiction."

"What do you like?" I asked.

"Romance and bestsellers," she said.

"Great!" I said. "You can't compete with the national chains in bestsellers, but you can be THE romance bookstore in Tulsa. You can carry a bigger inventory. Know all the authors. Serve tea. Be the expert. Learn your customers. Know what they like. Stock it for them."

But Margaret didn't want to do that. She chose to keep trying to do it all. She thought it would be enough to work hard, serve her customer and be the best that she could be. She kept competing head-to-head with chain bookstores and discount outlets. And her business failed.

Light approach works for California bookstore

It's possible for independent bookstores to compete against the chains and discount outlets, but they've got to be different.

One California used bookstore takes the light approach. As you enter the store a large sign warns you: "Every book in this store has been found to lack redeeming value by its original owner."

If you can make the owner laugh, he'll cut the price of your book in half. If you disagree with the price he has placed on a book, you can take a chance, double or nothing. He has a model airplane that flies around the ceiling of the store. If you can knock the airplane off its track with a dart gun, the book is yours free of charge. If you don't, you pay double. He also has a bin full of half-price paperback books. Each book has been cut in half. Customers have a good time in this store.

You can survive. You can do more than survive — you can be successful. Just don't go head-to-head against an established competitor who owns his position.

Bookstore positioning in Greenwich Village

The transformation of the Greenwich Village bookstore market in New York City shows how markets evolve and generate crackerjack positioning opportunities.

In the late 1970s the Village was heavily populated with general-interest bookstores, all competing with one another. Stores came and went. There was little to differentiate one from another.

Big bookstores arrive

Then the big bookstore chains arrived. In 1981 B. Dalton opened its outlet at the Village's busiest intersection. B. Dalton offers three floors of books and computer programs at that location. The store is well stocked with bestsellers, employs over 40 people and stays open most evenings until nearly midnight.

Barnes and Noble is in the same neighborhood. This store is

also owned by B. Dalton and sells bestsellers at a 30 percent discount.

So what happened to the small independent general-interest bookstores? They went away or they specialized. And the specialists are doing well.

Niche marketing works

The Village now has bookstores in many different positions. A shopper can find stores specializing in science fiction books, Russian and Italian books, and books published by university presses. There are stores selling gay-related books. Others sell feminist books.

Fred Wilson opened his store, Fred Wilson Chess Books, in 1979. Wilson says that more than 2,000 chess books have been published since 1475, and dozens of regular customers are building collections. Specialization gave Wilson the opportunity to develop a mail order business that provides 50 percent of his sales volume.

Foul Play Books of Mystery and Suspense points out that specialization makes it possible for the consumer to buy more intelligently. When you go to a specialist, you know you'll find a greater selection in your area of interest. You'll also find people who are knowledgeable about the specialty. Foul Play Books opened in 1980 and has done so well it's added a second location.

Guess what Biography Bookshop sells? The owners discovered that many people read nothing but biographies, so their store serves that market. Some patrons narrow their focus even further and just read biographies of kings and queens or literary figures or artists.

Find the unoccupied position

So you can see, there is room even in a highly competitive market. But you can only succeed if you're willing to let your established competitors have the positions they own and maintain.

You can succeed in a market dominated by large players. Like the 600-pound gorilla that can sleep anyplace he wants, the big boys can play anyplace they want. But, also like the gorilla, the big boys can successfully occupy a limited amount of space at any one time. So give them the position they've picked and look for a niche too specialized or too small to attract their attention.

The best way to find that niche is to learn more about your competitors' positions in the marketplace than they know. That's not as formidable a challenge as it may seem. We've seen how difficult it is to know one's own strengths and position from the inside. Your competitor has these same obstacles to overcome. So it may not be difficult for you to learn more than she knows.

To find a niche, do your research

When I was preparing to go into the country music business in Pueblo which I'll discuss further in Chapter 23, it wasn't hard to learn what the competition was programming. All I had to do was listen to the other radio stations. One station was playing rock music, another was a religious station and a third was Spanish language. The two other stations were programming all things to all people.

I knew what the stations were programming, but I didn't know how they perceived themselves or what the advertisers thought about the stations. Until I had that information, I would not know what viable market hole existed. Finding that information required digging, but it was available.

Ask questions

While I was listening to the stations I made a list of the largest radio advertisers. I joined the Chamber of Commerce and reviewed the list with the executive secretary. He allowed me to use his name as a referral when I contacted the leading radio advertisers. The advertisers were very cooperative. People are generous with their time when you are sincerely seeking advice. It didn't take many interviews for me to learn how each station's operation was perceived in the market.

I also talked to the managers of the competitive radio stations. A manager may not talk about her own operation but she will often talk about her competitors. After meeting with four managers I had a composite view of the market from radio station management's perspective.

Your situation will be similar. It won't take much effort to gain a broad perception of the existing market and the relative positions of the players. What you'll then need to know is how the players perceive themselves. And what do their customers think about them? These perceptions can differ from each other and may further disagree with the general public's analysis.

Company information is readily available

It's easy to find out what a publicly held company thinks of itself and what its plans are. A public company is required to bare all in its prospectus and to update that information with quarterly and annual reports.

Publicly held companies will generally send you their newsletters when you request them. These chatty little publications point with pride to the companies' accomplishments, report the companies' goals and tell how they plan to achieve them.

Privately held companies may be equally as cooperative. It's amazing what a company will send you if you ask for it. It's also amazing what they'll tell you over the phone, particularly if the company has an active public relations policy, or if you talk to somebody who doesn't know they aren't supposed to talk to you.

Even if a privately held company spokesperson won't talk about his operation, he'll often delight in gossiping about one of his competitors. Ask him who he considers to be his principal competitor and what he sees as that competitor's strengths and weaknesses. Then call the competitor and see what she says. Follow this process with enough companies, and you'll soon know more about the market than any other individual company does.

Study competitive advertising

Look at the sales brochures and advertising being used by your competitors. Make a list of the benefits they are offering. If they are trying to be all things to all people, what's their weakest claim.

See if you can find a niche that is not being covered. What competitive material does not say may be as important as what it does. Your intuition about the material will give you important insight into niche opportunities.

Shop the competition

Be a prospective customer. Visit the store, call for information, whatever is appropriate. Ask your friends to do the same. Compare notes. What seems to be strong points, or weak points in the competitive story? What's being emphasized or down-played in sales presentations? What's being overlooked? Once again, remember you're not looking for information to do battle head-to-head with an established competitor, you're looking for niche opportunities not being served.

Check public sources

Don't forget trade associations. As mentioned earlier, trade associations report on the general outlook for the industry in their publications. They also publish articles about individual companies. These articles will help you learn who your most formidable competitors are and what positions they occupy.

Those wonderful library research departments can help. They can search major newspapers for information on the specific companies you have under study. In addition, the inter-library loan system can locate and provide you with information from smaller publications. These publications often shine light on local issues not covered by television, the wire services or major metropolitan dailies.

Outside sources help, but nothing replaces you yourself wandering around and asking questions.

Talk to the experts

You'll find experts amazingly generous with their time. A devoted expert gets great pleasure from enlightening the ignorant. She'll expound at great lengths on the subtleties and intricacies of her area of expertise.

Be sure and prepare before you go calling on an expert. Plan your approach as a lawyer would for a cross-examination. Think about what you want to learn from the interview. Write out a list of questions you want answered. Be sure and study what information you have already found. If you display more than basic knowledge of the subject, your interviewee will know that your interest is sincere.

Keep an open mind

A good interview seldom follows the list of questions that you prepared. That's because your subject opens up and gives you her insight into the situation. Insight is what you want. Facts are available elsewhere. So let your interviewee talk, and forget your list.

Occasionally you'll trudge up a blind alley and run into a wall. Blind alleys are part of the game. When you hit a blind alley, let it go, pick another source and press on.

You can get all the information you need

If you keep at it, serendipity will occur. You'll run into a bit of luck. Somehow your investigation will come together and you'll find a new source or get an intuitive flash that provides a new perspective.

I was doing research for a restaurant client. There are not many subtleties in the restaurant market. Existing positions are reasonably clear. I was puttering around the market when I got lucky. Serendipity. I was referred to a gentlemen who had operated three successful restaurants in the market. Even more important, he had been out of the restaurant business for two years and had time to reflect on what he had done right and what he had done wrong. He gave me an objective market analysis only a successful and experienced operator no longer in the business could provide. His name was not on my original list of prospects. I would never have found him had I not been just wandering around the market.

You'll have enough competitive information when you've discovered who your major competitors are, what positions they occupy, and what they think about those positions. If you also know what they plan to do, so much the better. Now you can think about how you're going to be different.

Find Your Toy Surprise

Cracker Jack is different. It's a caramel-covered popcorn snack food mixed with peanuts. There are other caramel-covered popcorn products mixed with peanuts. But no other caramel-covered popcorn product mixed with peanuts also has a prize in every box. The prize is what makes Cracker Jack different.

You might even say that Borden sells you the prize and throws in the popcorn and peanuts.

Because Cracker Jack is different, it owns a position in the snack food world all its own. And because it owns that position, Cracker Jack commands a premium price. A large supermarket recently had Cracker Jack on sale for 23.5 cents an ounce. Crunch 'n Munch and Fiddle Faddle, products similar to Cracker Jack, were 19 cents per ounce.

You, too, have to be different if you want to command a premium price. If you're just like everybody else, nobody will remember who you are or what you do. You certainly will not be at the top of anyone's list.

Difference must be significant

Your difference must be a significant one that can be easily communicated. Consumers have their own priorities, and keeping up with nuances among a bevy of services and products that are virtually the same is not one of them.

Simple but not easy

Finding your unique factor sounds simple, and it is. But capitalizing on it is not easy. It's not easy because it requires sacrifice. Focusing on the development of your unique factor goes straight in the face of what we consider to be one our inalienable rights: the right to keep our options open, to cover all the bases, to do whatever we want to do, to not limit our choices, to be flexible.

To possess a crackerjack position, you must make the difficult and lonely decision to focus on a single element, your unique factor. It's a difficult decision because you must apply discipline. It's lonely because, by definition, you are by yourself when you are different.

But look at the rewards when you do make that choice. Soon you'll have a niche all to yourself. When the consumer needs what you offer, you'll be the logical choice.

It doesn't have to be a dramatic difference. It does have to be a difference that is easy for the consumer to understand and simple to communicate.

Domino's Pizza is different

Tom Monaghan began with a pizza parlor in Ypsilanti, Michigan. He wanted to grow. The question was how to do it. He knew he couldn't compete head-to-head with Pizza Hut. If he did, he would end up bloody and battered like Burger King. So Monaghan narrowed his focus. He selected a market segment that was not being featured by his competitors, a segment he could dominate with his limited resources.

Monaghan chose home delivery. Now home delivery wasn't new. This wasn't a dramatic, creative breakthrough. Other pizza parlors delivered. But no other pizza company focused all their efforts and resources on the home-delivery market. Nobody owned the home-delivery position in the customer's mind. As far as the consumer was concerned, the home-delivery position was open.

Monaghan saw this opportunity. He would leave the consumers who wanted to eat pizza in the store to his competitors. Domino's would focus on home delivery, within 30 minutes, guaranteed. Simple position, easy to communicate, and different from Domino's competitors, who were trying to do it all with in-store pizza, takeout pizza, delivery pizza, and other food choices.

Focus means giving up other options

When Monaghan made his choice to focus on home delivery, he sacrificed all his other alternatives. Domino's no longer provided in-store seating. Domino's no longer offered submarine sandwiches. Domino's was in the home-delivery business.

Monaghan redesigned his operation to accommodate the home-delivery focus. He went from three sizes of pizza to two. Domino's reduced the topping choices from eleven to seven. A cola was the only drink offered.

"Every time I dropped something," said Monaghan, "I made more money."

More effort focused on narrower choices leads to greater productivity and therefore higher profits. It's that simple. And it's that hard.

Niche marketing success requires commitment

The key to Domino's success was Monaghan's belief in what he was doing and his dedication to seeing it through. When you're being different you are, by definition, by yourself. When you're by yourself it's lonely and you sometimes look for cover. When you hit a bump in the road the temptation is great to go back to the way you were doing it before you came up with this crazy idea that nobody else seems to understand.

There must have been nights when Tom Monaghan gave serious thought to putting tables back in, adding beer, restoring submarine sandwiches, etc. Putting all his eggs in the home-delivery basket had to seem like a risky thing to do. Yet, if Domino's were to compete with Pizza Hut, he had no other option. So Monaghan stuck with home delivery, and the strategy was successful beyond his wildest dreams.

Many companies start out to focus on a single position but get off the track. It's easy to get diverted. There may be stockholders wondering what you're doing. The media will have comments to make. Industry experts may ridicule your activities. It's tough to hang in there. But hang in there you must if you are to achieve a crackerjack position.

Market segmentation dictates that there is no future for products everyone likes a little, only for things that some people like a lot. Products and services designed to offend no one will die.

Chrysler learns niche marketing

Chrysler is the number-three car manufacturer. As the number-three car maker, Chrysler must be different to compete with General Motors and Ford. If Chrysler is the same as its two giant competitors, it will fail.

Chrysler need look no farther than American Motors, a company it absorbed, to see what can happen. American Motors owned the four-wheel-drive vehicle market position with the established Jeep. Instead of focusing on this position and further strengthening it, American Motors threw its Jeep profits into a hopeless passenger car battle against the big three car makers. American Motors was destroyed and Chrysler absorbed the pieces.

Chrysler learned only part of the lesson. True, it made Jeep a division of its own. Unfortunately, it combined Eagle passenger cars with the Jeep. Guess which line makes money?

Since its rebirth under the leadership of Lee Iacocca, Chrysler's sales successes have been with unique vehicles such as the Jeep, mini-vans and convertibles. Instead of focusing its efforts on expanding these successes, Chrysler continued its fruitless battle against Ford and General Motors and poured money into unsuccessful diversification efforts. While Chrysler was pursuing this strategy, Ford perfected the Explorer. The Explorer is now neck and neck with Jeep and may become the established four-wheel-drive market leader.

Chrysler says it's learned its lesson.

"Jeep taught us the power inherent in a brand that's truly differentiated and consistent over time," said Laurel Cutler, Chrysler Vice President of Consumer Affairs.

Ms. Cutler also said that Chrysler had undergone a fundamental reversal in attitude toward consumer research on products and advertising.

"A good average score," said Ms. Cutler, "has become a directional arrow to nowhere. The only right numbers on a scale of 10 have become 10 and maybe zero. Polarization is good. When enough people love it, the people who hate it don't matter."

Chrysler now knows what you know. To survive in the constantly fragmenting marketplace, you must have a unique factor that clearly differentiates you from your competitors. Once you've got it, you don't let somebody take it away from you. You keep strengthening it.

Don't follow the leaders

You've got to find the element that will make you different. You start by eliminating everything that anybody else is spotlighting. Then look at what's left. It may be hard to see at first, but there's always something left.

There's always a hole. So keep looking.

The element doesn't have to be major breakthrough like the Chrysler mini-van or the Head ski. It can be as simple as Domino's home delivery, 30 minutes, guaranteed. Remember, Domino's didn't *invent* home delivery, they *focused* on it. Find an element you can focus on and communicate easily.

Supermarket chain creates and fills niche

Mike Vance is a creative marketing consultant. He once headed Disney University where the Walt Disney organization trains its employees. Vance illustrates the process of finding an element you can focus on with a story about one of his clients. The client was a supermarket chain developing superstores. The chain recognized that its existing medium-size stores were complicating this strategy and confusing their customers. The chain decided to eliminate this confusion by closing the medium-size stores. Closing the medium-size stores would create an opportunity for several convenience stores in each superstore's marketing area. The chain decided to fill this market hole themselves. It wanted its convenience stores to be different, so the company hired Vance to develop a creative solution.

Niche developed through creative approach

Vance and his colleagues began with the five-sensing technique. They considered what they could do to make the new convenience store different from the perspectives of smell, taste, touch, sight and sound.

Today the primary reason consumers go to a convenience store is to get something to drink. In line with that trend, Vance and company decided to feature coffee. They visualized making coffee so sensational that the store would not only get all the regular coffee drinkers, it would also capture consumers who didn't normally drink coffee. And they made it happen.

When you walked into this store, you not only smelled the fragrance of coffee freshly brewed in the normal way, you were also greeted by an exotic coffee espresso machine. Espresso coffee is brewed by forcing steam through finely-ground coffee beans. It's a simple process but very dramatic. You hear the "whoosh" of the steam going through the beans. You see the steam rise and smell the rich aroma of the finished product. You feel the warmth as you put your hands around the cup, and the dollop of whipped cream on top tickles your nose as you taste this delightful creation.

Consumers were, indeed, fascinated. They not only came back, they brought their friends. Customers even bought several expensive espresso machines.

One definition of creativity is arranging existing items in a new way. Espresso coffee machines were not new but they had never been featured in a convenience store before.

Similar tactic used by menswear chain

Another of Vance's clients developed a similar strategy. It was a chain of menswear stores. The client created a unique corner in each of his locations. This corner featured a particular type of menswear that was unavailable at the other locations. One store specialized in college clothes, another in athletic wear, and so on. Each store had regular menswear plus its special corner. It also had a reader board listing the other stores and their specialties. In this way the chain got the benefit of delivering the same basic product at each location but having a specialty as well. Sales improved at all locations.

Nugget casino does the opposite

You've got to be different. And one way to be different is to see what everybody else is doing and do exactly the opposite.

Shortly before I moved to Reno to manage KOLO radio station, Dick Graves opened the Nugget casino in Sparks, a suburb of Reno. At the time, the generally accepted method of attracting customers to a casino was to feature "name" entertainment. Graves believed this policy was getting to be too expensive because of the competition among the casinos for the limited number of proven attractions.

Food instead of entertainment

Graves took a different route. He knew that Sparks was a family town. And he knew the Nugget's success would depend on attracting the local Reno-Sparks populace on a regular basis.

Instead of building a showroom and booking name entertainment, Graves constructed several restaurants surrounding the central casino. The layout was similar to the food courts found in today's shopping malls, only on a much larger scale.

One restaurant specialized in pancakes, another in steaks and prime rib. There was a coffee shop, an oriental restaurant, an oyster bar, and the Golden Rooster Room specializing in chicken. The Nugget established a family atmosphere focused on food rather than entertainment. It occupied a new niche in the gaming industry and became quite successful.

World's worst art

It does pay to be different. Hardly a week goes by without another work of art being sold at an astonishing price by one of the world's major art auction houses. In Vancouver, British Columbia, things are done a little differently. Each year the British Columbia Paraplegic Foundation holds an auction of the "world's worst art." The foundation auctions about 150 works of art, which seldom bring bids over $2,000.

All year a committee from the foundation haunts garage sales looking for suitable items. Not just any painting will do. No paint-by-numbers or black-velvet pictures of Elvis are accepted. The foundation only buys oils, and they refuse to pay more than $5 for a single painting.

The foundation has its artistic standards as well. To be suitable for the "World's Worst Art Auction," a painting must display poor craftsmanship and planning, tasteless coloring or a silly subject.

The committee searches for paintings that have a head crammed into the corner because the artist ran out of room or a nude that leaves out hard-to-paint parts like hands and feet. They also like impossible scenes such as a sunset in front of a mountain.

Strategy builds on niche

The foundation delights in concocting ways to exploit its unusual auction. For example, the Foundation's most popular celebrity auctioneer is the legally blind curator of a library for the disabled. The curator conducts his auction waving his white cane in the air, pointing out the virtues of a painting he can't see. "Making a fool of yourself for a good cause is totally OK," he says.

The foundation also attempts to donate some of its works to famous art museums. When their gesture is rejected, the Foundation secures a valuable rejection slip attesting to the painting's authenticity as one of the "world's worst."

No competition

When you're different, you don't have much competition. As Norman Watt, art buyer for the "World's Worst Art Auction," says, "Very rarely do you miss a 'world's worst' because you arrived late at the garage sale."

So, ask yourself, how can you be different?

13 Pick A Niche

The information you've collected is now a bundle of complexities. Winston Churchill said, "Out of intense complexities, intense simplicities emerge." It's time to let that metamorphosis take place. You do that by getting the information up where you can see the relationship each bit of information has with the other. Then simplicities will emerge.

Positioning session

During the positioning session you review the material you've collected, see what opportunities that material opens for you, and make a decision about the direction to pursue.

A positioning session will take about half a day. The person with the authority to make the positioning decision must attend. Otherwise the process is an exercise in futility. The people responsible for taking action based on the position selected should also be there. It should be a workable group. Sometimes I've had sessions with two people. My largest session had ten people and that was too many. I believe a group of more than six people is unwieldy. With more than six people, somebody hides. Each attendee needs to participate. In addition to the participants, it's also helpful to have a person to record what occurs.

Three phases

The session has three phases. The first phase is the posting of information, the second is looking for relationships and patterns in the posted information, and the third is deciding on a position based on an interpretation of those relationships.

I use the storyboard technique to post the pertinent information where all the participants can see it.

Storyboarding

Storyboarding is a process developed by Walt Disney. An animated cartoon consists of thousands of individual drawings. Disney needed a method to keep track of these drawings as the cartoon unfolded frame by frame.

Disney studied Leonardo da Vinci's work. Da Vinci had discovered that placing one's work on a wall at eye level somehow stimulated creativity. Disney took that idea and applied it to his cartoons. He posted the drawings side by side on a board hanging on a wall.

The result was a storyboard that gave the cartoonists a picture of the evolving story and showed what needed to be done next.

Mike Vance took this idea and applied it to creative thinking. Vance calls his process "Displayed Thinking." Vance has numerous audio and videotapes, charts and associated products demonstrating his program. If you are interested in his materials, the address is: Michael F. Vance Inc., 16600 Sprague Road, Suite 120, Cleveland, Ohio 44130.

Storyboarding is an excellent method for selecting a crackerjack position.

Positioning session requirements

The ideal setting for storyboarding is a large blank wall covered in cork. It's also helpful if the wall is in a room where the cards can be left posted while you ponder the results of the session. This isn't absolutely necessary because you can take Polaroid pictures of the wall and its contents as you progress. And then you can ponder the pictures instead of the wall.

You'll need a supply of blank index cards. The process is easier to follow if you have different sized cards for different categories but that's not critical. Blank cards are no good without markers, so you'll want plenty of felt-tip markers with points big enough that the message written on the cards can be seen from anyplace in the room. If you're using a cork wall or large bulletin board you'll need push-pins. I find that masking tape works fine on the typical office sheetrock wall if that's what you are using.

If no walls are available, you can use one or more flip charts on easels. The disadvantage of flip charts is that you can't take a single idea or fact and move it to a different location on the overall wall as you can with cards. Also there is generally room for only one person to work at the flip chart at a time.

Each participant can take turns writing on a flip chart, but that's restrictive and cuts down on spontaneity. It's important for all of the participants to be actively involved in the process. Part of the involvement is filling out cards. The session will flow better if you use a storyboard wall.

When I hold a positioning session for clients, I encourage as much participant involvement as possible. "When the process is complete," I tell them, "I'm going home. You and your associates are left to refine and implement the plan that will carry out the strategy to achieve the position. So you can't just sit back and listen to a report. You've got to participate."

Simple process

The positioning session is a fairly simple process because most of the work has already been done. It's like a real estate closing.

During my real estate brokerage career, I was always amazed at how smooth most real estate closings are. Real estate ownership is the epitome of the American dream. The purchase of a home is the largest single financial transaction in most people's lives. So there is a lot of mystique associated with the actual transaction when papers are signed and money changes hands.

Yet the closing is generally dull. It's dull because all of the work has been done. Titles have been checked, financing arranged, problems worked out, etc.

So it is with determining your position. Most of the work is complete. You've collected the information and it's been steeping in your "medicine pouch." Now you just have to see what's there.

Why are you doing this?

It's helpful to review why you're doing this as you begin the session. Here are some opening questions to answer as you begin:

1. Why are you doing this?
2. What are your objectives?
3. What do you want to happen when this is over?
4. How will you know if you've been successful?

You want to have a clear idea of your motivation to keep the positioning exercise in focus. Answers to these questions provide that focus.

When I consulted with a regional supermarket chain, we began the positioning session with these questions. In answer to the question "Why are you doing this?" we reviewed the client's options:

1. Liquidate the company.
2. Continue doing what they were doing, which was slowly liquidating the company, although that wasn't the purpose of the strategy.
3. Sell the company.
4. Find a viable position.

If they had not already chosen the last alternative, we wouldn't have been in a positioning session. Still it's important to ask the questions and review the purpose of the exercise as you start the session.

So take one of those blank cards, write on it, "Why?" and post it on your wall. Then have your participants fill out cards stating reasons why you are going through this process and put those up there under the "Why?" card. Some topics may have subheadings and you can use other cards for those. The participants fill out the individual cards. The facilitator posts them.

Look at all the facets

You'll want columns on:

1. Why are we doing this?
2. Market Trends
   a. General
   b. Specific
3. Strengths
   a. Personal
   b. Company
4. Market Position
5. Competition
6. Potential Position

It doesn't matter in what order you proceed as long as you start with "Why?" and end up with "Potential Position." I generally follow "Why?" with "Trends." Sub-categories under "Trends" are "General," which is the outlook for the industry or profession under study, and "Specific," which is the market being examined.

The big picture

It's fun to get it all up on the wall where you can see it. When it's up there on the wall, you can sit back, look at the big picture, and pretend that you know what's going to happen even though none of us has any idea.

Looking at the big picture is essential. Major trends do have an effect on what you're going to do even when they seem very remote. For example, there's no question that the unification of

Europe into a single market is affecting all of us. It's important to take such trends into account.

Also, we tend to look at the broad trends with a certain detachment. That detachment helps us to be more objective. An objective viewpoint is useful as you look at your situation in greater detail.

Look at trends

Trends affect businesses in different ways. When I worked with the supermarket group, we looked at the population and development trends in the company's geographical market. That review showed us that growth was not sufficient to solve the declining sales problem. Therefore the positioning strategy had to focus on taking business away from competitors.

In contrast, geographical, population and development trends had very little effect on another client of mine, a manufacturing company that refurbished credit card imprinters. This company's market was not limited geographically. Instead it was technology that had changed the market dynamics. When credit card imprinters were relatively inexpensive mechanical devices, my client had been the only player in a small game. Now credit card imprinters are expensive high-tech machines that not only imprint the card but also capture information to be used in a variety of ways. The stakes are much higher and the big boys and girls want it all. Our challenge in this case was to find a niche that my client could control.

Cards keep things in perspective

Filling out cards and posting them on the wall keeps things in perspective. The problems don't seem as overwhelming when you can look at them in relation to other knowledge you have gained. Competitors are not as formidable when they are reduced to words on an index card.

The wall fills as the positioning process unfolds. First, you'll post the pertinent information. Then, as da Vinci discovered, with all of this information up on the wall, you begin to see patterns leading to possible positions.

Five differentiation possibilities

A business or service can be differentiated from its competitors in one of five ways:

1. Place
2. Price
3. Promotion
4. People
5. Product

All five contribute to the development of a unique position, but one element will be the focal point, the cornerstone of the crackerjack position. With all of the information on the board, you can now look at the patterns from each of these perspectives and see the possibilities in your particular situation. Which one looks the most promising?

How does the position fit?

One of storyboarding's most useful characteristics is its flexibility. As patterns suggest a potential position, you can start a new column with that position at the top. The information elements that give this position its potential can then be moved and placed in the column under the position heading. Now you can see how these elements fit. How do they look together? How do they feel? What problems do you see? What are the pluses? The minuses?

When the position is right and good and true, you'll know it. You'll know it just like the French painter Pierre Auguste Renoir knew when he had completed a portrait of a nude. When asked how he knew, Renoir replied: "I just keep painting until I feel like pinching. Then I know it's right."

You'll know your position is right but you'll need to live with it awhile to make sure it fits. Just let this new concept mellow in your "medicine pouch" for a time before developing a strategy. The time varies. It could be as little as a few hours, as long as a few weeks. You'll know when you've waited long enough.

Value of outside help

You can do all of this yourself. You can do it faster with the help of an outside consultant who has been through the process a number of times. You can reach just such a person by writing the address or calling the number you'll find on the last page of this book.

While your crackerjack position is fermenting, we'll look at some case histories to see how the positioning selection process has worked for others.

A Marvelous Mixture of Mirth, Magic and Message

In the early 1970s I discovered that I have a speaking talent. The *Book of Lists* reports that 41 percent of 3,000 Americans surveyed said that speaking before a group was their number-one fear. Contrary to the survey, I found speaking in public to be an exhilarating experience. I wanted to do more of it. And I wanted to get paid for speaking to groups.

"Crackerjack positioning" is defined as the act of putting a person or enterprise of striking excellence in a marketplace location or condition of advantage. In Chapter 5, I told you about my search for the strengths that would make me a crackerjack speaker of "striking excellence." While I was making that search, I needed a "marketplace location of advantage." Here's how I found one.

Good market for professional speakers

In the early '80s the market for speakers grew rapidly. Market and industry fragmentation created a demand for associations to serve the new specialized market segments. Associations have meetings. Meetings require speakers. More associations holding more meetings means a demand for more speakers.

So the market was good. In a good market, supply rapidly fills demand, particularly when a market is as easy to enter as professional speaking. Soon meeting planners were awash with speakers. And I was faced with the challenge of differentiating myself from all the other new entrants. So I looked at our old friends: Place, Price, Promotion, People, and Product.

Place

"Place" is not generally a significant factor in the speaking industry. Meetings and seminars are typically held in resort or metropolitan locations. Most of the participants, including the speakers, come from someplace else, so a speaker can operate from anywhere that air transportation is available.

There is a strange mystique that surrounds the expert from out of town. For some reason, when a presenter comes from more than 200 miles away his program is perceived as more credible than a similar performance from somebody local. This aura is particularly strong if the expert comes from an exotic metropolitan area like New York City or San Francisco. I had no desire to move to New York or San Francisco, and it didn't seem to make that much difference anyway. So "Place" was not a positioning opportunity for me.

Price

"Price" is also not a significant factor in hiring a speaker. When a meeting planner wants a celebrity or specific expert, she's willing to pay the going rate. If the planner is simply looking for an adequate keynote or after-dinner speaker with no extraordinary name value, she has a vast field of virtually interchangeable speakers available. Consequently, the planner can name her price.

Promotion

"Promotion" wouldn't work either. A meeting planner's career rides on his selection of speakers. Any mistake he makes is highly visible. Consequently, meeting planners hire speakers whom either they have heard or somebody whose opinion they respect has heard and recommended. Extensive advertising and promotion will not significantly influence that basic decision process.

People

"People" is one of the two key differentiation factors in professional speaking. The other is "Product," which we'll come to shortly. Celebrity speakers draw crowds. The celebrity may or may not be able to speak very effectively but that's not important. He's booked because the hardware dealer from Des Moines wants to go home and tell his friends that Walter Cronkite spoke at his convention. Cronkite exemplifies the established celebrity. "The CBS Evening News" was consistently rated number one over the other major network news programs when Cronkite was the program's anchorman.

Instant celebrities

In addition to established celebrities like Cronkite and former presidents, there are instant celebrities who speak to groups. Andy Warhol said that the day will come when everyone will be famous for fifteen minutes. Instant celebrities are famous for fifteen minutes. They're like fads. An event creates an instant celebrity, who rockets onto the scene, burns brightly and quickly disappears.

Disgraced politicians often become instant celebrities. The Watergate break-in and subsequent coverup cost Richard Nixon the presidency. It also spawned a large school of instant celebrities. More than thirty Nixon administrative officials, campaign officials and financial contributors pleaded guilty or were found guilty of breaking the law as a result of Watergate. Many of them became instant celebrities who wrote books and went on the speaking circuit.

Experts

In addition to celebrities and instant celebrities, meeting planners hire accepted experts in a particular field. Buck Rogers and Tom Peters are two examples.

F.G. "Buck" Rogers was with the IBM Corporation for thirty-four years and retired as vice president, marketing, with responsibilities for IBM's worldwide marketing activities. Rogers wrote *The IBM Way*, and *Getting the Best Out of Yourself and Others*. According to *USA Today*, Rogers is one of the five most requested speakers in America.

Tom Peters co-authored *In Search of Excellence* with Bob Waterman. Waterman and Peters were management consultants with the firm of McKinsey & Company. *In Search of Excellence* became the best-selling business book in history. Since then Peters has written other books, including *Passion for Excellence* and *Thriving on Chaos*. He has become a recognized expert on dealing with the changing business environment and frequently speaks on the subject to corporation and association meetings throughout the world.

Product

I was not a celebrity, an instant celebrity or a recognized expert. "People" as a differentiation factor was out, which left "Product." I had to develop a product that was different.

My wish was to become a humorist. Earlier I mentioned the problems associated with that desire. I was not a natural born humorist. I couldn't even tell a joke. The public speaker closest to being a natural humorist was probably Mark Twain, and even Twain didn't find humor easy. When he was asked how he wrote humor, Twain replied, "It's the easiest thing in the world. You sit down at a table with paper and pencil and you write it down as it occurs to you. Writing humor is easy, it's that 'occurring to you' that's hard."

Fortunately, learning to tell a joke or story is not as difficult as creating humor. Telling a joke is more a developed skill than a creative exercise. It simply takes practice to acquire effective timing. Still, learning a skill takes time, and there were already speak-

ers who could do an excellent job of telling a joke. I needed
something more.

Roy Hatten

I was searching for that "something more" when I went to my first
National Speakers Association convention. At the convention,
Roy Hatten delivered a presentation on the use of humor. What
made Roy Hatten unique, however, was not so much his use of
humor as his magician's ability. Roy was a talented magician. And
it occurred to me, "Hey, I can do that. I won't be as good as Roy,
but I'll be different. I'll be a speaker who can use magic to support
my message."

I approached Roy and he was very helpful. He spent hours
talking with me at the convention. Roy became my mentor, supporting and advising me for several years afterward until his
death.

Magic provides a product niche

When I got home from the convention I discovered Sandy
Rhodes. Sandy is a fine magician with a love for the craft and a gift
for teaching. He taught me how to create an illusion and helped
me develop a basic repertoire of magical illusions that I could use
as a speaker.

The strategy worked. I now had a product that was unique. I
had first narrowed my field of competitors from some 1,000 motivational speakers to less than 500 motivational/humorous speakers. With the addition of magic, I was now one of about a dozen
motivational/humorous/magician speakers.

My natural talent as a motivational speaker, mixed with my
developing ability to tell a joke and my basic skill as a magician,
made me different. So I titled my talk "A Marvelous Mixture of
Mirth, Magic and Message."

The Associated Clubs liked the concept and the title. In 1982
they added me to their recommended speakers list. The Associ-

ated Clubs are booking agents for Knife and Fork, Metropolitan and Executive Dinner Clubs throughout the country. Each of these clubs meets about six times a year for fellowship, dinner and a program. Over the next three years I spoke to more than fifty clubs from coast to coast and border to border. Traveling the country I learned that I didn't really want to be an after-dinner speaker constantly on the road performing one-night stands. Sometimes you have to experiment to discover what fits. Building on what fits is a key part of crackerjack positioning.

Ralph Archbold as Ben Franklin

Ralph Archbold did not want to be on the road doing one-night stands either. Ralph has built a crackerjack position in the speaking profession by doing what fits for him. Archbold was a photographer in Dearborn, Michigan. As a photographer he had flexible working hours so when he was asked to play Ben Franklin at a local historical village Ralph thought "Why not?" and took the job. The village management gave him a ten-minute script and a costume, and turned him loose. The pay was good, the hours were short and Ralph was having fun, so when schools and garden clubs started asking him to visit, he thought, "Maybe I should keep doing this."

Ralph was developing a position based on "People." He was playing Ben Franklin. Whereas this role differentiated Ralph from other speakers, his position was still weak. Any actor in costume and makeup could do what Ralph could do.

Ralph adds "Product"

Ralph added "Product" and strengthened his position. He had learned his ten-minute speech was not enough to sustain his role so he began researching Ben Franklin. The more he learned the more he realized that Franklin's beliefs and principles were easily modified to fit today's environment. Ralph began using Franklin's material to tailor a message for his clients. He says, "The character is the vehicle for the message."

Ralph now looks like Franklin. He is balding on top, has let his back hair grow long and wears Ben Franklin eyeglasses. When Ralph appears at speakers' conventions he is always in costume. So you never think of Ralph Archbold without thinking of Ben Franklin.

Move to Philadelphia

As his Ben Franklin reputation grew, Archbold was frequently asked to travel to Philadelphia and speak to meetings and conventions. Ralph saw this demand as an opportunity to further strengthen his position by adding "Place" to "People" and "Product." Although he knew only one person in Philadelphia, he gathered up his family and moved there. The first two years were a struggle but now Ralph is established as THE Ben Franklin in Philadelphia.

Ralph says, "If you bring your group to Philadelphia, you need to have Ben Franklin. If you don't have Ben Franklin you really should go to Kansas, it's cheaper." And if you want Ben Franklin then you want Ralph Archbold.

Expanding on crackerjack position

Ralph has further capitalized on "Place." He lives near Independence Hall in Philadelphia. Ralph likes to walk to work so he focuses on meetings in that area. He works with nearby meeting facilities, many of which include his material in their marketing packets. Others recommend him to groups that have booked their location.

Ralph encourages his clients to bring him on as a surprise. He suggests the client call him when the servers start picking up dishes from the main course. He can then leave his front door, walk to the meeting place, and be ready to go on when dessert is done. Following his program Ralph will stay and visit with the group as Ben Franklin.

"Price" completes the strategy

Since Ralph confines his efforts to the Philadelphia area he does not spend time traveling. Consequently, Ralph's fees are lower than those of speakers who have to consider travel time when setting prices. This gives Ralph a "Price" advantage over other speakers in addition to his "People" (Ben Franklin), "Place" (Philadelphia), and "Product" (research and tailoring) niche.

The crackerjack positioning process is versatile. It applies to an individual developing a personal career as well as businesses establishing positions in diverse markets.

Your Friendly Neighborhood Travel Agency

My first positioning strategy client was a travel agency. The agency had one office operated by an owner and two agents. The goal was to find a crackerjack position that would differentiate this agency from the other eighty-five travel agencies in the market.

Future bright for travel industry

Trends show that the general outlook for travel agencies is good. Fewer families are taking automobile vacations because the interstate highway system is more than thirty years old and is in disrepair. Instead, they are going directly to destination points such as Disney World. Families need travel agencies to help make these arrangements.

Airline travel will continue to increase. People want to save time. There is no suitable railroad system. And the aforementioned decline in the interstate system discourages automobile travel. Airline rates are complex and change rapidly. It's impossible to buy an airline ticket at the lowest available rate without using a travel agency. Global market development encourages international travel in spite of high costs. The population is aging. As families mature and children leave home, parents have both the time and the discretionary income to travel.

Agency located in soft market

For these reasons the future looks good for travel agencies. However the short-term outlook in Oklahoma, where this travel agency was located, was not so bright. Oklahoma's economy was soft following the early 1980s oil bust. Travel agencies were struggling to survive and competition was fierce. My client could close his office or merge with another agency, but he didn't want to do either. Instead he wanted to develop a crackerjack position that would allow him to prosper.

No obvious unique factor

After looking at the general and specific market situation, we reviewed the agency's customer base. Records were sketchy but there seemed to be no commonality. Clients came from all walks of life, all different businesses and all over the geographical market. What the customer base did reflect was that the agency was adept at journeyman travel agency work. They did a good job of serving basic travel needs.

One of my client's employees was intimately familiar with Mexico but so were a lot of competitive agents so that was not a unique factor. Competitive firms ran the gamut from one-person enterprises to large agencies with multiple locations and dozens of agents. Some agencies specialized in corporate travel, others focused on tours or cruises. But the majority were still operating in the "all things to all people" mode. Research completed, we held a positioning strategy session.

Search for niche

Remember the list of possibilities? Place, Price, Promotion, People and Product?

"Price" wouldn't work. If anything it would work against my client. Although airline ticket prices are generally the same anyplace, large-volume agencies can sometimes get discounts. Cruise and tour specialists can also get special rates in their areas of specialty.

"Promotion" was not a possibility in the total market. Large agencies could easily out-spend my client. These agencies were also in a better position to tie in with advertising media and give away free trips as special promotions.

What about "People"? The agency's staff were pleasant and friendly with an interest in service. They did not reflect a highly sophisticated office, nor did they possess highly specialized knowledge. The agency enjoyed constructing custom trips for clients and small groups but this was not a unique travel agency skill. My client and his agents were well traveled, but there were veterans in the business who had taken more cruises, seen more countries, etc. For my client, "People" was not a differentiating factor.

"Product" was not an alternative. There were already specialists in tours, ski trips, cruises and corporate travel. We couldn't find an available product specialty that would be profitable.

Neighborhood travel agency

That left "Place." And "Place" was the crackerjack positioning opportunity. My client was the only travel agency located in an older section of town that is quite proud of its heritage. The residents and businesses like to set themselves apart from the balance of the metropolitan area. The agency office was located in a shopping center named after the neighborhood. My client's agency also carried the neighborhood name. My client and his people were from small towns. Their warm homespun personalities fit the image people had of the neighborhood.

The crackerjack position was open to be the neighborhood travel agency. It wouldn't be necessary to directly compete with the big guns or the product specialists. Instead, the agency could spend its time and resources being an active member of the local community. It could take advantage of the small-town atmosphere and build small-town loyalties by working with its neighbors.

During our session, this crackerjack positioning opportunity arose from the index cards charts as if unassisted. Crackerjack positions do that. As the idea unfolds, it becomes more obvious and grows stronger. It takes on a life of its own.

Agency is sold

My client agreed a position as a neighborhood travel agency in this particular area was a viable position. He joined the neighborhood merchants' association, made plans to change his hours to fit neighborhood needs, and began soliciting opportunities to speak to neighborhood groups. Before this strategy could be implemented, another travel agency made him an attractive offer and he sold the business. The purchaser turned the agency into a satellite office.

Miss Laura's Social Club

Miss Laura's Social Club was located in a building that housed a bordello during the early days of Fort Smith, Arkansas. The Donrey Media Group has its headquarters in Fort Smith, and in 1963 the company purchased the abandoned historical structure to keep it from being demolished.

The building was placed on the National Register of Historic Places in 1973. The only bordello to be so honored. Restoration began in 1983. Every effort was made to duplicate the spirit of the early 1900s, when Miss Laura's had functioned as a bawdyhouse.

Restaurant leased

Donrey leased the restored Miss Laura's to a restaurant management company and it was opened as a club and restaurant in 1984. Unfortunately the lease didn't work out. Donrey found itself in the restaurant business after numerous attempts to find another suitable operator were unsuccessful. Under Donrey's management Miss Laura's Social Club became a Fort Smith landmark and tourist attraction. However, it wasn't a financial success.

Why seek a position?

In 1989 I met with Donrey management to explore alternatives. Donrey is a billion-dollar communications company with successful newspaper, cable television, broadcast and outdoor advertising operations throughout the country. Operating a restaurant was outside its area of expertise, and the associated problems were demanding valuable executive time and energy that could be better spent on its primary business. My first suggestion was to purchase a large padlock and close the restaurant. Donrey management agreed that was a viable alternative but wanted to make one more effort to establish a profitable restaurant, which could then be leased to an outside operator. If successful, this action would protect a historic structure, provide a tourist attraction for Fort Smith, Donrey's headquarter city, and turn a loser into a winner.

So we went looking for a crackerjack position that would help improve Miss Laura's financial performance. There was some talk about returning the operation to Miss Laura's original business. However the authorities are not quite as permissive as they were in the early 1900s, so that idea was abandoned.

Collect information

My first step was to collect information. I interviewed people to find out Miss Laura's perceived position in the community. I surveyed civic leaders, competitive restaurateurs, present customers, former customers, restaurant employees and the park service staff at the Fort Smith National Historic Site. I also went to the library and researched industry magazines and trade publications.

Positioning session

Research completed, I met with the two executives supervising Miss Laura's for the positioning session. We looked at the survey results. Under "Survey" I listed "civic leaders," "restaurateurs," "customers," "non-customers," "employees," and "National Park Service."

Market perception

I told them what I had learned. The market perceived Miss Laura's first to be a tourist attraction, and second as a special-occasion restaurant. Local residents went to Miss Laura's for birthdays and anniversaries because of its unique environment. They also brought out-of-town visitors to see Miss Laura's. However the restaurant was judged to be too high-priced for the quality of food and service received, so many customers did not eat there regularly.

The atmosphere, although interesting, was thought to be too sterile and intimidating for a restaurant. Customers would talk in whispers as if they were in a museum. Miss Laura's was also regarded as unreliable because the restaurant frequently changed operating hours. Some respondents considered Miss Laura's to be a Donrey Media Group toy. One person told me he was glad Donrey owned it because the company could afford its losses.

On the chart under "Perceptions," I listed: "tourist," "special-occasion," "high-priced," "service," "food," "location," "sterile," "intimidating," "dull," "inconsistent" and "toy."

Competitors

Next we agreed on the ten restaurants that were direct competitors of Miss Laura's. All ten were relatively high-priced operations suitable for special occasions. Three of the restaurants were private membership clubs. Two of those were country clubs and the third was a downtown luncheon club that also served dinner.

Three of the competitors were located in historic structures. One of these was an Italian restaurant, owned and operated by a local Italian family. The second was a German restaurant, owned and operated by a local German family, and the third was an upper-scale yuppie restaurant featuring a popular bar and a broad menu.

The direct-competitor list also included a seafood restaurant on the banks of the Arkansas river, a large family restaurant run by one of Fort Smith's well-known and successful restaurant operators, a gourmet restaurant established in a downtown high-rise hotel and, finally, an established steak house located in a barn on the outskirts of Fort Smith.

Place, Price, Promotion, People, Product

As you recall, a business or service can be differentiated from its competitors by one of five means:

1   Place
2. Price
3. Promotion
4. People
5. Product

We looked at Miss Laura's from each of these perspectives.

Place

"Place" includes the physical location of an enterprise as well as the structure in which it operates. At Miss Laura's, "Place" was a "good news, bad news" situation. The good news was Miss Laura's was an authentically restored bawdyhouse listed on the National Register of Historic Places. The bad news was the structure was located in an industrial area next to a railroad track and rendering plant. A switch engine was usually parked on the track, not far from the restaurant. The switch engine's diesel engine was noisily running most of the time.

Miss Laura's was also beyond comfortable walking distance from downtown so luncheon customers had to drive to get there. Miss Laura's wasn't close to anything but the switch engine and was not on the way to anywhere. "Place" was not the answer.

Price

"Price" was also not a possibility. Miss Laura's was a two-story structure built to be a hotel, not a restaurant. Preserving the historical integrity of the structure created restaurant operational inefficiencies as well as space limitations. Design made it impossible for Miss Laura's to become a low-price volume restaurant.

We briefly considered a high-price gourmet restaurant operation. There were problems with that option. A high-price gourmet restaurant would require an additional capital investment in both equipment and people. Even if Donrey chose to spend the money, Miss Laura's record indicated that the market probably wouldn't support a high-ticket gourmet restaurant. So we discarded that idea.

Promotion

"Promotion" had been tried. Miss Laura's was owned by a media company that could, and did, use its own companies to promote the location. A great deal of time, effort and money had been spent publicizing the unique history of Miss Laura's. The restaurant carried out the Victorian theme. Pictures of some of the original occupants of Miss Laura's were hung on the wall. Historical documents unique to the operation, such as personal health certificates of the "ladies" were also displayed.

A magnificent stained-glass portrait of Miss Laura decorated the bar. The bar offered drinks with period names in unusual glasses, some with garters attached. Souvenirs, including postcards, shot glasses, playing cards, drink tokens, etc., were sold on the premises. During dinner a hostess dressed as Miss Laura wandered about the restaurant answering questions and telling the story of the structure to the customers.

Donrey knew how to promote, and promotion had made Miss Laura's a major Fort Smith tourist attraction. The Chamber of Commerce received as many inquiries about Miss Laura's as they did about Old Fort Smith and Hanging Judge Isaac C. Parker's

Courtroom. Miss Laura's had the tourist trade, but that wasn't enough to support a profitable operation. And the Fort Smith tourist market was shrinking. Visitor count at the Fort Smith National Historic Site of Old Fort Smith was steadily declining. It had been a long time since John Wayne rode out of Fort Smith as Rooster Cogburn in *True Grit*. Many cities and towns are attempting to capitalize on a nostalgia theme by restoring their historic districts. Consequently, Fort Smith is not the unique historical attraction it once was.

Tourist attractions tend to discourage local repeat business. If you lived in Fort Smith, how many times would you like to look at a restored bawdyhouse and listen to "Miss Laura" expound at length on the history of the building? Typically, a Fort Smithian would bring visiting Aunt Bee by Miss Laura's to see the building and have a drink. Sometimes they just looked at the building and didn't even have a drink. We know that the market perceived Miss Laura's meal prices to be too high for the value received, so it's no surprise that the party would then go to dinner elsewhere. Miss Laura's needed something more than "Promotion" to attract repeat local business.

People

"People" didn't provide an answer. Miss Laura's was owned by a large corporation. The restaurant was run by hired management, not owners. Three of Miss Laura's principal competitors were owned and operated by well-known local families. Owners greeting patrons gave those restaurants a flair Donrey could not duplicate.

Another "People" positioning possibility was to hire a superior chef. The chef would then become the featured attraction. This alternative had the same problems as the high-price gourmet choice. In addition, if we spent money promoting the chef and he left or was hit by a truck, our investment vanished. So we eliminated that option.

Product

"Product" had to be the solution. In the restaurant business, "Product" is the food that you serve and how you serve it. We looked at what people ordered at Miss Laura's and discovered that the customers preferred red meat. Prime rib was the biggest seller, followed closely by two types of steak. Forty-two percent of the entrees sold were red meat.

This record seemed to conflict with America's increasing health consciousness. It's well documented that the public's concern about heart disease has led to a decline in beef consumption because of beef's high fat and cholesterol content.

Further research showed us, however, that whereas its true that beef consumption has declined approximately twenty percent since 1978, Americans still eat more beef than chicken and fish combined. On an edible weight basis, Americans eat almost seventy pounds of beef a year, compared with 43.4 pounds of chicken and fifteen pounds of fish, according to the U.S. Department of Agriculture.

Furthermore, restaurant industry studies report that quality beef is still the entree of choice at upscale restaurants. The decline in beef consumption is occurring at home and at lower-priced steakhouses featuring tenderized utility-grade meat.

Miss Laura's geographical location was also a factor in their customers' preference for red meat. According to *Restaurant News,* most of the country's steakhouses are located in the South. Arkansas is a Southern state.

The steakhouse located in a barn on the outskirts of Fort Smith was the only one of Miss Laura's direct competitors that featured red meat. Although this restaurant still referred to itself as a "steakhouse," its menu offered quail, lobster, shrimp, ham and chicken in addition to steaks.

Niche opportunity as steakhouse

So a crackerjack positioning opportunity began to come into

focus. The position could be built on Miss Laura's strengths and take advantage of competitive weaknesses in the Fort Smith restaurant market.

Miss Laura's Social Club was an established tourist attraction. Modest promotion would keep that market. The positioning opportunity for generating repeat local patronage was in the product offered. Sales records told us that Miss Laura's existing customer base preferred beef. Steak and prime rib fit the Miss Laura's Social Club rough-and-tumble image. Miss Laura's was already perceived as a high-ticket restaurant. Industry studies told us that consumers patronizing upscale restaurants wanted quality beef. Featuring beef would not require additional equipment or exceptionally skilled staff. The only direct competitor that had a quality steakhouse position had seriously weakened that position by adding a number of fish and fowl items to its menu.

For all of these reasons, the door was open to build on Miss Laura's tourist attraction image and capture a crackerjack position as THE steakhouse in Fort Smith.

Final solution: a large padlock

To be successful, however, a crackerjack positioning strategy must be consistent and carried out by competent and committed personnel. Donrey's inexperience in restaurant management made it difficult to find such personnel. Within six months Miss Laura's went through three management changes. Donrey management decided they had made their final effort to establish Miss Laura's as a viable operation and it had failed, so they purchased a large padlock and closed the restaurant.

Either Price or Value, Not Both

There is an additional factor to consider as you develop a strategy to communicate your newly selected position to your target market. That factor is how your positioning strategy fits the relationship between price and perceived value.

A consumer makes a decision to invest her money based upon her perception of the value of the product or service she receives in exchange for her money. The better the value, the more likely she is to spend her money.

Definitions

For the sake of comparison I'll use the following definitions:

> "Price" is the amount of money the consumer spends to acquire the product or service.
> "Value" is the perceived worth to the consumer of the product or service he bought.
> "Profit margin" is the difference between what the consumer pays for the product or service and what the supplier spends to make the product or service available.

Price/Value matrix

The consumer has a perception of the value he'll receive for the price he'll pay for every business with which he comes in contact. That perception develops from a variety of sources: his actual experience, advertising, word of mouth, driving down the street, whatever. The contact is made and a perception results. That perception will fall into one of the four quadrants on the following matrix:

Low Price High Value	1	2	High Price High Value
Low Price Low Value	4	3	High Price Low Value

Creating value can be complex. For our purposes, it is sufficient to say that a supplier must spend money to create value; and generally the higher the value, the more money he spends to create it.

High Price/Low Value

The supplier would like to be in the High Price/Low Value (#3) quadrant and still have the consumer shop with him because his profit margin would be greater. However, a customer won't make a purchase in the High Price/Low Value quadrant if she's aware of any other choice. The free enterprise system creates competitors. Competitors provide choices. Today's sophisticated communications systems soon inform the consumer of those choices. When the consumer learns of the choices, she abandons the High Price/Low Value quadrant business, and unless the business adjusts, it fails.

Low Price/High Value

A business can operate in the Low Price/High Value (#1) quadrant for brief periods of time. That's what mark-down sales, introductory prices and loss leaders are all about. If the business attempts to operate in the Low Price/High Value quadrant all the time, its profit margins will be too low to cover its costs, and ultimately the business will fold.

Often businesses are led into the Low Price/High Value quadrant by a demanding public. Both the consumer and the business know that choices are available. The consumer makes actual or implied demands. The business capitulates, particularly during periods of otherwise stagnant or declining sales. The business doesn't want to lose a single sale so it stretches its capital to satisfy the consumer's demands. What little profit margin remains now goes to pay for the increased activity required to satisfy all the demands. Ultimately there's no margin left and the business collapses.

Viable quadrants

Since an informed consumer won't make purchases in the High Price/Low Value quadrant, and a business can't survive in the Low Price/High Value quadrant, only positions in the High Price/High Value (#2) quadrant or the Low Price/Low Value (#4) quadrants are viable long-term alternatives.

Peking Garden

Two contrasting restaurant operations under the same ownership demonstrate this principle in action. The first restaurant is Peking Garden. Peking Garden is a quality Chinese restaurant. It offers a large variety of authentic Mandarin, Szechuan, Hunan and Cantonese cuisine. The restaurant provides a pleasant oriental atmosphere and excellent service. Exotic drinks in unusual glasses are also available. When you go to the Peking Garden, you expect these services. You also expect to pay for them, so Peking Garden falls in the High Price/High Value quadrant.

The owners of Peking Garden recognize that, while today's society may enjoy fine dining on special occasions, it also wants the convenience of fast-food. To satisfy this desire, Peking Garden's owners created an entirely different operation. They opened Egg Roll Express.

Egg Roll Express

Egg Roll Express, as the name suggests, provides Chinese food fast. Egg Roll Express has several locations, so the customer doesn't have to drive far to purchase takeout Chinese food in a hurry. Egg Roll Express offers little service and the price is low, so Egg Roll Express is positioned in the Low Price/Low Value quadrant.

Notice the Peking Garden people didn't build a drive-in window on the side of their fine restaurant. Nor did they call the new operation "Peking Express." The owners recognized that the customer must have a clear position in his mind of both operations. When the consumer desires a fine Chinese meal chosen from a variety of alternatives, and to have that meal served in a pleasant atmosphere, he will pick Peking Garden. When he wants Chinese food in a hurry that he can take home and eat while he watches television, he opts for Egg Roll Express. There is no confusion in the consumer's mind what each restaurant provides. The perceived value is consistent with the price.

Strategy must be consistent

Business enterprises can succeed with positions in either the High Price/High Value quadrant or the Low Price/Low Value quadrant. To be successful, however, the operation must be consistent so the consumer is not surprised. When the consumer is surprised, she becomes confused.

The consumer doesn't like to be confused. The customer does

not shop at stores where she's afraid she may be confused. Instead, she goes where she knows she'll get what she expects. Once you select your position, your positioning strategy must not confuse the consumer. Everything must support the position the business already has in the consumer's mind.

Wal-Mart

Wal-Mart has a consistent position in the consumer's mind. Wal-Mart is a Low Price/Low Value company. Wal-Mart customers expect to pay low prices for products and services they perceive as having an adequate but relatively low value, and they are not disappointed. In-store signs state Wal-Mart's position: "Always the Low Price. Always."

Wal-Mart's Low Price/Low Value position has made it the nation's largest retailer. Founder Sam Walton, at his death one of the world's richest men, illustrated the Wal-Mart image. You never saw a picture of Walton where he wasn't wearing a Wal-Mart baseball cap. Walton even wore his cap when President George Bush came to Bentonville, Arkansas, where Wal-Mart is headquartered, to present him with the Freedom Medal. Walton sent the message that Wal-Mart is the common store for the common customer.

Wal-Mart walks a narrow line convincing customers that, whereas Wal-Mart prices are low, the products have satisfactory value. Subtle touches like wider aisles, recessed lighting and carpeted apparel departments give customers a warmer feeling than they get from other discounters.

Wal-Mart's small-town strategy

Sam Walton built Wal-Mart by establishing stores in small towns. Often retailers in these towns tried to ignore the new giant in their midst and did business as they always had. Like it or not, low prices overcame hometown loyalties, and those stores went under.

Wal-Mart points out that when they build a new store in a locality, their purpose is not to wipe out the local retail community. The Wal-Mart goal is to establish a new retail hub that keeps dollars from going to nearby metropolitan areas. The company has testimonials from 300 chambers of commerce to prove their point. When local retailers accept the reality that the new Wal-Mart in their town has forever changed the business environment and develop strategies to cope with that change, then they can and do succeed.

Successful co-existence with Wal-Mart

Viroqua, Iowa, is a good example. When Wal-Mart announced that it was going to build a store in Viroqua, Fred Nelson, who owned Nelson Mill & Agri-Center, didn't just buy a padlock for his front door and give up. Instead, he went on a fact-finding trip to the nearest Wal-Mart. Nelson learned that competing with Wal-Mart on price would be impossible, so he looked for a position he could occupy. Seeing that Wal-Mart's size made it impossible for their stores to provide individual attention, Nelson decided to focus on providing top service to the local farmer, his best customer. First, Nelson abandoned health and beauty aids and adjusted his inventory to avoid direct competition in areas he knew Wal-Mart would dominate. Then, Nelson expanded his farm-supply department, broadened his returns policy and extended his operating hours. He and his staff know their customers, call them by name and provide services Wal-Mart is too big to supply. Nelson Mill & Agri-Center more than survived; the store's sales increased by almost twenty percent, and profits remained steady.

Wal-Mart leaves niche opportunities

Other Viroqua merchants learned from Nelson's example and established their own unique market positions. A local fabric store recognized that Wal-Mart would win on fabric prices so they reduced their fabric inventory, expanded into accessories, started a custom sewing service and added a wedding and prom dress department. All these services were unavailable at Wal-Mart. A

Viroqua shoe store proprietor realized his typical customer would now buy at Wal-Mart so he went after local sports teams and retirement home residents. He now brings samples to schools and homes and delivers the final order himself. He offers discounts to teenagers. He keeps size and phone number files on his senior citizen customers and stocks extra-wide shoes for their needs.

Wal-Mart's consistent focus on dominating the Low Price/Low Value quadrant created opportunities in the High Price/High Value quadrant. Viroqua merchants exploited these opportunities by adding value to their enterprises with increased services including product variety. Everybody won — Wal-Mart, the local retailer and, most of all, the consumer.

Miss Jackson's

The key to success in the High Price/High Value quadrant is service. Service is the reason Miss Jackson's succeeds in today's price-conscious business environment. Miss Jackson's is a High Price/High Value specialty shop. Miss Jackson's began more than eighty years ago as a lingerie shop located in a jewelry store. The store is now housed in a three-story building in a fashionable shopping center.

Customer service is vital

Miss Jackson's High-Value position is created not only by the products it carries but also by the services it provides. Nelle Shields Jackson established the store's reputation by treating each customer with the same hospitality she would provide in her own home. Every customer is offered a soft drink, a cup of tea or coffee and, sometimes, even a light lunch.

Miss Jackson's customers are not rack shoppers. A patron with serious interest in a particular garment is invited to a private presentation room to view accessories or other possible selections. Miss Jackson's customers want privacy. And they want free gift wrapping and free delivery. They want service and they get it. And when a mistake is made, Miss Jackson's fixes it.

Miss Jackson's makes mistake

A number of years ago Miss Jackson's ran an advertisement shortly before Valentine's Day featuring a costume jewelry bracelet with the inscription "I'm damn good!" on it. The price was less than $20. "Great idea," I said to myself. And I went to Miss Jackson's to buy one. A lot of other people also thought it was a good idea and the supply was sold out when I got there. However, the sales associate said that another shipment of bracelets would be in the store on Saturday morning.

"I'm going out of town over the weekend," I told her. "Valentine's Day is not until Monday. Would you save me a couple of bracelets and I'll pick them up Monday?"

"No problem," I was informed. And off I went for the weekend.

On Monday I returned to Miss Jackson's to pick up the bracelets. My friendly sales associate was on vacation and there were no bracelets. I was irritated, so I wrote Bill Fisher, owner of Miss Jackson's, the following letter:

> Dear Mr. Fisher:
>
> Last Wednesday I went to your store to purchase Valentine bracelets for my wife and daughter that I had seen advertised by Miss Jackson's. The bracelets are inscribed "I'm Damn Good!" Judith waited on me and was most cordial as she explained that you had sold out of these bracelets but another shipment was expected that night. She told me that the bracelets would be on sale Friday and asked if I would like to reserve two.
>
> "Yes, indeed," I told her. "But I'm going to Kansas City on Friday. Can you hold them until Monday?"
>
> "Of course," she said. "They'll be waiting for you on Valentine's Day."

Monday I received a message that somebody named Marilyn from Miss Jackson's had called my office on Saturday. "Hmmm," I thought, "probably to tell me the bracelets are here."

When I arrived at your store Monday afternoon, I was told that Judith was on vacation and nobody knew anything about holding two bracelets for me. I made a scene over this shabby treatment. Then Marilyn appeared to tell me that she had called my office on Saturday and, since I wasn't there, why, she just went right ahead and sold those little old bracelets that had been promised to me.

Now, Mr. Fisher, there wasn't any question about our agreement. I was promised that two bracelets would be waiting for me on Monday, but they weren't. It's obvious that when there was a demand for the bracelets on Saturday, a meaningless gesture was made to contact me. Since I wasn't in my office on Saturday morning, the bracelets were sold. Apparently Miss Jackson's customer service policy is to break a promise when there's a chance to make an immediate sale. In the future I shall plan accordingly.

Sincerely,

Donald W. Reynolds Jr.

Miss Jackson's fixes it

I quickly received a hand-delivered personal letter of apology from Bill Fisher, together with a box of Godiva chocolates. When another shipment of bracelets arrived, Mr. Fisher delivered two at no charge with his compliments. And when the sales associate returned from vacation, she, too, wrote a personal letter of apology.

That is High Value, created by the combination of product and exceptional service Miss Jackson's consistently delivers. Of course, you pay a High Price for that High Value, but you know that going in to the transaction, so there are no surprises. Miss Jackson's High Price/High Value position has enabled the store to not only survive the oil-related depression in Oklahoma but also to show profit increases every year.

Only one Miss Jackson's

There's only one Miss Jackson's. The focus required to create that High Price/High Value position and the market size required to support it do not permit more. Maintaining a consistent position in the High Price/High Value quadrant demands a dedication to quality. It's difficult to maintain that dedication in multiple locations.

Stanley Marcus wrote the book

When Neiman Marcus was owned and operated by the Marcus family in Dallas, Texas, the store occupied a position similar to Miss Jackson's. Stanley Marcus wrote two books, *Minding the Store* and *Quest for the Best,* which tell you what it takes to maintain a High Price/High Value position.

Unfortunately, Stanley Marcus left Neiman's many years ago after the company was sold to the Broadway-Hale group. Neiman Marcus is currently owned by General Cinema, which may explain why the store is no longer an example of how to be a High Price/High Value operation. Now that it's a division of a publicly held company and has branches in eleven states, Neiman's fails to deliver on the promise of service and quality you could once count on.

Neiman Marcus fails to follow up

Recently at Christmas my family met in Hawaii to spend the holidays with my father, who now lives there. My daughter lives in the Dallas area and ordered several presents from Neiman Marcus to be gift-wrapped and shipped to her in Hawaii. In mid-December a strange package addressed to an unknown family in North

Carolina arrived in Hawaii from Neiman Marcus. My family returned the package to Neiman's with an explanation that nobody with the addressee's name lived there or was expected to visit. Christmas came and went with no further shipment from Neiman's. After Christmas, my daughter called Neiman's and learned that not only were the packages not delivered prior to Christmas, but the merchandise, which had been ordered well in advance, was now sold out.

"Sorry," said Neiman's, "but nothing can be done. We'll issue a credit."

Neiman Marcus made no effort to right their wrong. They did not suggest replacing the missing merchandise with similar, possibly more expensive, items. Nor did they offer to send a letter or small gift to the intended gift recipients accepting full blame for the snafu. Nothing but "Sorry. We'll issue a credit" from Neiman Marcus.

Contrast that attitude with an action taken by Stanley Marcus in 1964 following a pre-Christmas fire that virtually destroyed the Dallas store. Marcus knew that a number of wedding deliveries were scheduled for the day after the fire. Since all the bridal and attendants' gowns were stored in the bridal salon, they were either smoke-or water-damaged. Marcus rented a suite of rooms at a hotel and called in the entire wedding garment stock from his Fort Worth and Houston stores. He notified every bride to come and make a new selection. Neiman's re-outfitted fifteen bridal parties without losing a single bride.

Difficult to maintain position

Neiman Marcus is in transition from a position in the High Price/High Value quadrant to one in the High Price/Low Value quadrant. Many department stores have fallen into this trap, which helps account for the flurry of bankruptcies in the trade. Department stores are pressured by discounters. Many are publicly owned and stockholders expect profits. Rather than beef up service to justify their high prices, the stores do just the opposite.

They cut back on service to maintain profit margins. When the consumer sees that she no longer gets the service she expects, she concludes that the value she anticipated is also gone and switches to the discounter. She doesn't get much service at the discounter, but she doesn't demand much because she's paying a lower price. And the original department store vanishes.

People are not stupid.

If Neiman's wants to regain its High Price/High Value position, it will have to learn to be as responsive as Miss Jackson's. Neiman Marcus executives should read Stanley Marcus's books.

L.L. Bean

Or they could study L.L. Bean, the mail order house in Freeport, Maine. L.L. Bean not only stands by its lifelong advertised policy, "If you're not satisfied for *any* reason, we will return your money," it bends over backward to serve a customer.

A friend of mine, who is a longtime Bean customer, was invited to go hunting. At the last minute he discovered his Bean boots were tattered beyond repair. He made a panicky weekend call to Freeport, where your L.L. Bean call is never put on hold, 24 hours a day, 365 days a year. Could he get the boots, and would they be the right size? Bean normally has you draw a line around your foot to determine size. During the weekend the company's facsimile machine was locked up, so my friend couldn't send a drawing.

"Not to worry," said the Bean representative. "We'll express you *two* sizes. You return the unused pair. Good hunting."

Now that's service.

The airline industry

Many airlines are suffering the consequences of an inconsistent positioning strategy. Until deregulation, government protected routes allowed airlines to enjoy positions in the High Price/Low Value quadrant. Each airline provided modest service at high fares. Seats were scarce on popular routes. Airlines made money. Government deregulation in 1978 changed all that.

Airlines flooded into each others heretofore protected territories. Seats were suddenly plentiful. Fares plunged. Airlines came and went. Food and service became fodder for stand-up comedians.

One popular story had an airline passenger checking her baggage at the ticket counter.

She told the agent, "I want this bag to go to London, this one to Buenos Aires, and that one to New York."

"We can't do that." said the agent.

"Why not?" replied the passenger. "You did it last week."

The public now perceives airlines to be operating in the High Price/Low Service quadrant. Thanks to the complex rate structure each passenger is convinced everybody else on the plane is paying a lower fare than he is. Consequently consumers choose to stay home or drive. Seats are empty. Airlines rush into fare wars to fill them and place themselves in the Low Price/High Value quadrant. The public buys the seats but the industry loses money. In 1990-91 airlines lost $6 billion.

Southwest Airlines

One airline has been profitable for 20 consecutive years. Southwest Airlines achieves that record by consistently operating in the Low Price/Low Value quadrant. The airline does not maintain an expensive reservation system so you don't get an assigned seat. Your meal will be a bag of peanuts. If you change airlines you must transfer your luggage yourself.

What you do get from Southwest Airlines are frequent, on-time, point-to-point flights at rock-bottom prices.

There are no surprises on Southwest and they make flying fun. Airplanes may be painted to look like Shamu the killer whale or the Texas State Flag. In the early 1970's flight attendants wore hot pants and Southwest president Herb Kelleher has been known to fly on St. Patrick's Day as a leprechaun. Consumers trust Southwest to deliver what it says it will. The airline's load factor, the percentage of seats occupied, was recently 67% compared to an industry average of less than 59%.

Southwest Airlines positioning strategy

Southwest keeps its operation simple and cheap by focusing energy on the few services it does provide. The airline avoids direct competition with its huge competitors by flying from smaller airports with less traffic. In California, for example, Southwest operates between Oakland and Burbank rather than San Francisco and Los Angeles. Since a Low Price/Low Value strategy requires high volume to be successful, Southwest will not enter a new city unless it believes the market will support eight flights per day.

Southwest flies one aircraft, the fuel- efficient Boeing 737. This policy simplifies fuel costs, aircraft maintenance and flight crew training. It also helps the airline turn its planes around in 15 to 20 minutes. The industry average is 45 minutes. Consequently Southwest can fly one passenger one mile for 6.8 cents. A passenger mile costs American 8.8 cents and United 9.6 cents.

Competition

Southwest's position is solidly established and it now has little to fear from competition. Major airlines invested their capital in huge aircraft, complex maintenance facilities and sophisticated reservation systems. They also operate from expensive airports. These investments make it impossible to compete directly with Southwest's lower operating costs. The only way a major airline could compete with Southwest would be to start all over with the same narrow focus on a single position that Southwest has maintained. Even then it's doubtful the competitor would be successful because Southwest is established in its position and is not about to abandon it.

It's also impossible for Southwest to compete directly with

major airlines on long hauls. That's just fine with Southwest. The company has witnessed what happens to short-haul airlines that get greedy. An operation is successful flying between places like Dayton and Detroit. The executives get bored, buy 747's and start competing with the big people flying to London and Honolulu. The airline gets wiped out like General Custer did when he attacked the entrenched Sioux warrior position.

Consistent strategy maintains position

Southwest Airlines, Peking Garden, Egg Roll Express, Wal-Mart, the Viroqua merchants, Miss Jackson's and L.L. Bean succeed in part because they understand their crackerjack positions. They accept what's required to maintain those positions and deliver what's expected. The consumer is not confused or surprised. Your crackerjack position must be just as clearly located in either the High Price/High Value quadrant or the Low Price/Low Value quadrant as these merchants. And your strategy must be just as consistent with your position if it's to succeed.

No Trust, No Chance

Your crackerjack position will create trust. You must be trusted by the consumer if you're to have a chance at transacting business with her. "Trust" means more than the consumer believes you're honest. Honesty is generally taken for granted.

Consumer believes in you

The trust issue here is that the consumer believes that you'll be able to satisfy her need in an acceptable manner should she decide that she has a need. If she doesn't have that belief going in to the process, you'll never get the opportunity to display what you can do. It's unlikely, for example, that my daughter will ever order another gift from Neiman Marcus. Neiman Marcus has betrayed her trust. She no longer believes they will be able to deliver it in a timely manner. Her experience supports that belief. Not only will she not buy anything else from Neiman Marcus, neither will any member of the family that was involved with this incident. Trust is gone.

On the other hand, my hunting friend will never, ever buy a pair of boots or virtually any other kind of hunting equipment from anybody *but* L.L. Bean. He not only trusts that they will be able to deliver, he knows they will go the extra mile because they already have.

L.L. Bean will be asked to serve again. Neiman Marcus won't be. And if you aren't asked to serve, you can't make the sale. It doesn't matter how good you are, you've got to get asked.

Four questions in a transaction

A buyer asks four questions in every transaction. The key question involves trust. The purchase of a pound of coffee demonstrates how the process works. Suppose you ran out of coffee this morning and a morning cup of coffee is an important part of your daily routine. Because it's important to you, you'll buy more coffee before tomorrow morning. Buying a pound of coffee isn't a major investment so you won't give it much conscious thought. You'll probably stop at your convenient supermarket, select a can of coffee, pay for it and take it home. Consciously or unconsciously, you asked yourself a question at each step in the transaction.

Here are the questions:

1. Do I want coffee?
2. Who do I believe can provide me with coffee?
3. Can the source I thought could satisfy my need actually satisfy it?
4. Do I want the coffee *now*?

Every transaction involves these four questions. The buyer decides he has a need. The buyer believes that the seller can satisfy the need. The seller has an opportunity to provide a solution to the need. And the buyer decides to accept the proposed solution.

As a seller, you can help the buyer through this process. You can help the buyer see her need, and you can show how your solution satisfies the need, and you can help the buyer decide to accept your solution. But only if you get the chance.

The key question involves trust

You won't get the chance if the buyer doesn't first believe that you have the capability to satisfy her need should she have one.

This is the crux of crackerjack positioning, so I'll repeat it. The buyer must trust that you have the ability to solve her problem or satisfy her need before you'll get the opportunity to present your solution. No trust, no opportunity. That simple.

Clear position creates trust

In this increasingly complex world, a consumer has many alternatives. She's constantly bombarded with conflicting messages about those opportunities. As a result, she is often confused. A confused consumer hesitates. The simpler your message and the clearer your position, the easier it is for the buyer to remember you when she has a need for what you provide.

The key is to make your position simple and clear so that the consumer understands that you can and will produce results should he have a need for what you do. If you do a thorough job of establishing your position, you can preempt all the other players and be the only logical choice when the need arises.

Red Adair puts out oil field fires

Red Adair has such a position. When there's an oil field fire, the people in charge call Red Adair. They call him because Red Adair is the man who puts out oil field fires. Newspaper and magazine articles have been written about him. Feature movies tell of his exploits. He's written an autobiography, *The American Hero*. When it comes to oil field fires, Red Adair is the man to call. The goal of your strategy is to give your crackerjack position the same preemptive power Red Adair has. When people need what you provide, you're the only choice.

Super Bowl watch parties

Every January the champions of the American Conference and the National Conference of the National Football League play each other to decide who's king of the football hill. The game is called the Super Bowl. Much hype and hoopla go with the Super Bowl. Each year the media work to build it into an event upon which it appears the future of the world will depend. Hotels overflow. Tickets are scalped at outlandish prices.

In spite of what the media would have you believe the world would probably survive without the Super Bowl. Former Dallas Cowboy running back Duane Thomas put the hype in perspective when he asked, "If this is the ultimate football game, why are they going to play it again next year?"

The Super Bowl may not be the ultimate game but it does attract more interest than any other single sporting event. That interest results in television watch parties. There is no better food for a watch party than pizza. And guess who the watch-party hosts call to deliver pizza?

Domino's is the first choice

Domino's position of trust as THE pizza company that provides home delivery within thirty minutes, guaranteed, preempts the other choices. Competitive pizza companies *may* be able to deliver on time but you *know* Domino's will, so why take a chance? Super Bowl Sunday is usually Domino's best sales day of the year.

Need for cataract surgery

Recently I had to have cataract surgery. My family has a history of glaucoma and cataracts so I have been monitoring the condition of my eyes for several years. The cataracts had grown large enough to affect my sight. There was no other choice. If I wanted to see, I had to have the operation.

There was no reason to doubt that my regular eye doctor could accomplish this surgery. He assured me that he could. And he said that he performed the operation frequently. Still, I only get two eyes so I wanted to check around before selecting a surgeon.

Doctor's crackerjack position creates trust

When I asked friends and acquaintances for their recommendations, one name was frequently mentioned. I made an appointment with this doctor. His staff was efficient. The doctor was confident, reassuring and obviously in love with his work. His fee was sixty-six percent higher than my current doctor. I checked some more. I found another recommended surgeon whose fee was only forty percent higher than my original doctor.

Still, the more I inquired, the more the first doctor's name kept coming up. Then I went to my internist for a minor unrelated problem. My internist is an M.D., a medical doctor. The frequently mentioned eye surgeon is a D.O., a doctor of osteopathy.

The two disciplines are very competitive and seldom have good words to say about each other. I was sure my internist wouldn't recommend the D.O. When I asked him, his first suggestion was an M.D., then he mentioned the D.O. When I told him that the D.O. had already examined my eyes, my internist enthusiastically recommended him. He warmed to the subject and went into detail on the D.O.'s history and experience. My internist told me that any objective M.D. would admit that the D.O. was clearly "Top Gun" in cataract surgery.

Guess who I chose?

I chose the D.O., of course, and the operation was highly successful. My original doctor could probably have done the surgery, but I *trusted* the D.O. to be able to handle anything that might come up during my operation. I trusted him because he was positioned as the expert in cataract surgery.

I later found out that because I was relatively young to have cataracts, the process was a bit different than it would have been in a more typical case. No problem for Top Gun. He had performed thousands of these operations and studied the latest methods with experts as far away as Europe. My situation might have been a problem for somebody else. Then again, it might not have been. Who knows?

Who wants to take the chance?

In the normal course of events, I would never have considered the D.O. since my medical experiences had always been with M.D.s. The D.O.'s position was so strong that it overcame my traditional medical preferences and gave him the opportunity to convert me to a patient.

I trust my internist, and his recommendation calmed any uneasiness I had due to my ignorance about osteopathy and its practitioners. It did not matter that the D.O.'s fee was higher. When you're positioned as number one in your field, your fee should be higher. The key issue was the belief the D.O. could perform the operation.

Abundance of choices

The trust issue is critical in today's marketplace. People have more choices available than ever before so it's difficult to make buying decisions. Just look at the cereal aisle in your supermarket. Have you ever seen so many choices?

Recently I counted one hundred and seventy-six different choices in a supermarket cereal aisle. One hundred and seventy-six! No consumer is even going to look at one hundred and seventy-six boxes, let alone do the research necessary to make an educated decision on which breakfast cereal to buy. Even if they did, there are new brands on the aisle every day. In addition to standards like Corn Flakes and Cheerios, there are fad cereals. There are nutrition fads such as oat bran as well as cereals named after Saturday morning television characters and popular movies. Pebbles from the Flintstones is a current offering. We've had Batman and Teenage Mutant Ninja Turtle brands. There are cereals for holidays like Christmas Lucky Charms. There's Breakfast With Barbie, named for the fashion doll. We probably had Hula Hoop cereal when Hula Hoops were the rage. Recently there was an Addams Family cereal. It was sugar coated, of course, and in the shape of headless dolls, skulls, and Thing, a character from the movie.

It's easy to make fun of the myriad available cereal choices clamoring for our attention at the supermarket. It's not so easy to laugh when we realize that the same situation exists in most industries and professions.

Consumer will do modest research

Everywhere there is an abundance of choices and a constant flow of new entrants. The consumer has neither the time nor the interest to thoroughly research all the alternatives and make the wise choice. At best, the consumer is going to poke around a bit and then make a decision.

My eyes are important to me. Even so, I didn't talk to every single doctor or thoroughly investigate every possible solution to my need for cataract surgery. I explored the field until I was comfortable with the choices and picked what I perceived to be the best surgeon.

No doubt there are eye surgeons who could have done a satisfactory job that I didn't consider. I didn't consider them because their position was not strong enough to get them on my final cut list. You've got to make the list to be a contender.

Just as I decided to have surgery from an eye surgeon whom I trusted, people select cereal brands from manufacturers they trust. In recent years the two leading cereals have been Kellogg's Frosted Flakes and Kellogg's Corn Flakes. People trust Kellogg and they understand corn flakes, with or without sugar frosting.

Trusted source gets the business

When oat bran became a hot item because research indicated it would reduce cholesterol, consumers didn't rush out and buy one of the many new cereals that raced onto the market trumpeting high oat bran content. Instead, they chose a brand that has been made from whole grain oats for almost half a century, Cheerios. They trusted General Mills and they understood Cheerios. So they made it the number-one seller.

The same selection process goes on in your business or industry. To be considered, you must be trusted. So as you work to implant your crackerjack position in the minds of your targeted market, remember that it must build trust first. Your prospect must believe that you will produce if called upon. The ideal situation is to have a trust position so strong that consumers consider you to be the only choice. The best way to build that position is to be simple, honest and clear.

Focus Your Resources

Crackerjack positioning strategy is intended to teach a potential customer that you can deliver what that customer wants when she decides she wants it. When you have that trust, you have the opportunity to be of service. No trust, no opportunity.

Focus on your niche

Crackerjack positioning strategy is like a running play in football. In a running play all of the team's players, its resources, are focused on creating a hole in the defense that the ball carrier can run through.

As you can see from the following illustration, each player has a specific contribution to make if the play is to be successful. And these contributions must be made in a timely manner. If they're not, the offense is confused, chaos results and the defense has no trouble stopping the play.

Positioning strategy follows the same process as a successful football play. You focus all your resources on implanting your position in the mind of your targeted market. Just as every player makes his contribution to the football play, each resource makes its contribution to establishing your position. To be effective, all the resources, like all the players, must work together. There can't be any mixed messages.

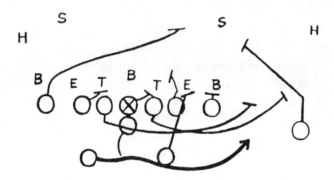

Keep it simple

The simpler your position is, the easier it is to implant. So make your position as simple as possible. Start by following the advice of Michelangelo Buonarroti.

When asked how he could create a sculpture as magnificent as David, Michelangelo answered, "I carve away everything that isn't David."

So carve away everything that isn't necessary to explain your position. Define your position in as clear and concise a statement as possible.

Seven words or less

Look at outdoor advertising billboards. They'll help you shorten your positioning statement. Whizzing down the freeway at sixty miles an hour doesn't leave much time to read outdoor advertising signs. Effective outdoor advertising, therefore, must have a short message. Seven words or less is ideal.

Seven words or less is also an ideal length for your positioning statement. It keeps you focused, and you can tell people at a chamber of commerce cocktail party what you do before they lose interest. Attention spans are notoriously short at chamber of commerce cocktail parties.

Use a concise position statement

When people ask me what a positioning strategist does, my first answer was, "Help people discover, accept, develop and capitalize on a unique position in their marketplace." That's fourteen words, a bit long. So I continued to carve away, and now I define the essence of what I do with one word. The word is "Focus."

Here are examples of concise position statements:

"Toy Surprise Inside!" is printed on the Cracker Jack box. That's a three-word positioning statement.

Wal-Mart says: "Always Low Prices, Always."

At Miss Jackson's it's "There's Only One Miss Jackson's, Celebrating Eighty Years of Excellence."

A business that understands its position can state it in less than a dozen words. If you can't do that, you don't understand your position. Keep working on it until you do.

Pictures increase position statement impact

Adding an illustration to your position statement increases its effectiveness. The Children's Medical Center in Tulsa combines a child's drawing of a smiling sun with its positioning statement. The statement, written in the primitive printing style of a first-grader, says, "Helping Kids Get Better."

Children's Medical Center

Helping Kids Get Better.

Consistent strategy builds position

For over sixty years the Children's Medical Center has specialized in the treatment of children, adolescents and their families. "Helping Kids Get Better" states that position simply and clearly. Its strategy is consistent with its position. Children's Medical Center patients come from professional referrals, and not the public at large. Still, it's important for the public to have a good feeling about the Center.

No holiday is more important to kids than Christmas. For the holiday season, the Center erects a giant drive-through display of huge toys, inflated balloons and Christmas lights. The display grows bigger every year and attracts visitors from miles around.

The Children's Medical Center understands its market. Its position statement and the strategy supporting that statement are examples of crackerjack positioning at its best.

Check what you are doing

When you understand your position and can state it in a very few words, preferably seven or less, and when you have settled on a name that reflects what your position is, then check your operation to make sure all of your activities are consistent with the position.

Examine everything you are doing and ask this question, "Does this activity help me clearly establish my position?" If the answer is "Yes," keep on doing it just that way. If the answer is "No," then ask yourself these questions: "Can this activity be eliminated altogether?" If not, then ask, "How can this activity be modified to support the position?"

Don't skip anything. Stand across the street and look at your physical location. Does it fit? Is it clean? Is the location consistent with your position?

Go inside. How about your interior decorating? Does the decor fit the position? Be sure to check your graphics. Look at your logo, advertising, exterior signs, stationery and calling cards.

Call your business on the phone. How does it sound? Have somebody else call and make a few simple requests. See how they are handled. Get a mystery shopper to drop in.

Every aspect of your business that comes in contact with the public must consistently reflect and communicate your position.

Tie your strategy to prospect's perceptions

Seven-Up did that with the Un-Cola campaign. When most people think of a soft drink, they think of a cola because cola drinks outsell all the other types put together. So Seven-Up related its product to what was already in the consumer's mind, that soft drinks are colas. Seven-Up promoted itself as the "Un-Cola" and sales increased dramatically. Any positioning strategy that takes advantage of what's already in the prospect's mind has a much higher possibility of being remembered.

Cracker Jack is perceived as a delightful product. People associate it with carefree youth. They remember getting a prize and eating the caramel-covered popcorn mixed with peanuts. Cracker Jack has been around since the late 1800s. It's well established in the consumer's mind.

I want people to remember what I do and have a good feeling about it, so I give away Cracker Jack whenever I make a talk. I have stickers with my name and logo, which I can put on Cracker Jack boxes so I can use them as business cards. I give away Cracker Jack at Christmas and on special occasions. When friends and acquaintances see me coming down the street, they want a box of Cracker Jack. I buy a lot of Cracker Jack.

People may not remember my name but they remember Cracker Jack. When they remember Cracker Jack, they remember the story I tell about Cracker Jack's unique position in the world of snack food and how it got that position. Then they remember what I do.

See if you can find a similar relationship between what you do and an existing perception in the mind of your prospect. As

Seven-Up found, it's a lot easier than trying to get an entirely new message into that crowded brain.

Assume nobody knows what you do

Regardless how you do it, you want to tell everybody who needs to know what your position is. Don't assume that anybody will notice. People are fighting their own battles and they're too preoccupied to worry about your new position. Remember those thousands of advertising messages that pour down on people every day? There's simply too much information out there.

A member of my Toastmasters Club is a certified public accountant. She recently entered private practice after being with the Internal Revenue Service for several years. Now that she's in the real world, she's amazed at how many people have no idea what a certified public accountant is or does.

So if you are going to assume anything, assume that nobody knows and nobody cares what your position is or what it's going to be. That's the only assumption that won't get you into trouble. Make a list of who needs to know. Include your employees. They talk to folks, and your employees need to be able to explain in that same thirty seconds or less what you do. Your current customers need to know. They probably contributed to the development of your refined position, so keep them informed.

Tell your competitors

If you've done a good job of positioning, you'll want your competitors to know. You'll want them to know because your position now makes you different from your competitors. If they are as sophisticated as you are, they'll send business your way that they can't handle but know you can. Naturally, they'll expect you to do the same.

RKG Associates Inc., a $1 million real estate consulting firm in Durham, North Carolina, gets job referrals by sending its company newsletter to its competitors. The newsletter is published semiannually and includes information on RKG projects, regional news and economic issues. The first two mailings brought two profitable jobs and lots of leads from competitors.

Tell everybody

You'll want industry experts to know about you. In fact, you want to have anybody who might talk to anybody else about what you are doing to know your position. You may be going after a specific market that doesn't include many of your acquaintances, but you can never tell when one of them will have the opportunity to recommend you. So be sure your friends and acquaintances know what you do.

Have you ever worked on a nonprofit board or committee with somebody and not have any idea what they do for a living? They may not know what you do either, so tell them.

Often we take for granted that people know our business. Sometimes they don't and are too embarrassed to ask. Tell 'em. The best way to communicate your position is to tell people in person. But that's fairly inefficient because it takes time to talk to everybody. The next best way is to get news coverage. Articles and news stories have much more credibility than advertising.

Get outside help to refine strategy

You've gone to a lot of trouble to create a unique position, so what you do should be newsworthy. Consider contacting a public relations firm to help you with your news releases unless you have a flair for journalism. Even if you do have journalism skills, it's probably a good idea to use a professional. She can give you an objective perspective.

Most cities have a number of good free-lance public relations writers who can help you put your information together so that it will be interesting. Newspaper editors or broadcast news directors can recommend somebody. They know the people who do a good job of bringing them information in a usable form.

You can invest as much money as you feel is justified in professional public relations. It will be relatively inexpensive to have a free-lance public relations writer prepare and distribute a simple news release for you. Larger firms can prepare extensive public relations campaigns.

Keep in mind the purpose of the strategy

Whatever you do, remember that all facets of your strategy should focus on the single goal of communicating your unique position to your market as clearly as possible.

Name
Supports
Position

Nothing is more basic, or more important, than the name of your product, service or company. Ideally your name will tell exactly what you do. It's clear what Children's Medical Center does. Egg Roll Express obviously doesn't sell Mexican food. If your name doesn't tell what you do, at least keep it from confusing people.

What's a "Carlon"?

It's not hard to confuse people. Several years ago I started a property management company and named it "Carlon Corporation." The name was a contraction of "Cowardly Lion" from the *Wizard of Oz.* I had decided that I was like the Cowardly Lion, that what I needed to be successful was courage. "Carlon" expressed that decision. Of course nobody understood that but me.

Not content with creating a strange name that required lengthy explanation, I went on a spiritual quest for the perfect lion illustration for the Carlon Corporation logo. You can't imagine the time and effort I wasted searching for the ideal lion. I made one printer so mad he quite rightly refused to do business with me ever again.

What did "Carlon Corporation" tell the prospect about my

property management company? Nothing, absolutely nothing . . . which may explain why that business was not very successful.

Positioning Strategists

I learned. My firm name now is "Positioning Strategists." My logo is a group of similar boxes with one highlighted.

The logo says and shows what I do. I still have to explain what a positioning strategist does because it's not a common profession. There may not be any others. So I explain what I do with my fourteen-word positioning statement, but I don't have to first explain the name and then what I do.

Don't let ego determine name

One of Tulsa's most successful commercial real estate brokerage firms is named "Tulsa Properties, Inc." How refreshing! There's no question what this firm does. If you're interested in a property in Tulsa, contact Tulsa Properties. Makes it simple, doesn't it? Tulsa Properties' logo is a drawing of the downtown Tulsa skyline, which makes it even clearer what they do.

Most real estate brokerage firms are like law firms: The name

Tulsa Properties, Inc.
11010 East 51st St. So.
Tulsa, Oklahoma 74146

DON REYNOLDS
POSITIONING STRATEGIST

reflects the ego of the owners. A friend suggested that professional firm names should express what they do such as "Dewey, Billum and Howe" or "Engulf and Devour." Good idea, but most of the time the title of the firm is simply a collection of proper names.

Stock brokerage firms also use proper names. It's the accepted norm in the profession. When a friend of mine and several of his associates started a regional firm a few years ago, they recognized that a stock brokerage firm's name should sound like it's been there forever and project a quality image. They named the firm, "Parker, Ford & Associates." None of the originating partners were named either "Parker" or "Ford." They realized that these names reflected companies with quality images. By associating themselves with the quality images already in the customer's mind, they were able to project the impression they desired. Plus, they avoided the necessity of reprinting all their material every time someone either joined or left the firm.

Physicians names say what they do

Physicians are not generally considered marketing geniuses, but many have learned that their firm's name should reflect what they do and not their ego. My telephone book lists names like: Ear Nose & Throat Clinic, Eye Center, Facial Cosmetic Surgery Center, Heart Institute, Foot Clinic, Cancer Care Associates, Sports Medicine Center, Arthritis Surgery Center, New Life Weight Control, Back Institute, etc. You look at those names and you have a pretty good idea what those physicians do.

Relate name to prospect's perceptions

Whenever possible, pick a name compatible with your prospect's existing perceptions. That's what Procter and Gamble did with Head and Shoulders shampoo. One of the reasons Head and Shoulders continues to be a leader in a highly fragmented product category like shampoo is because its name expresses what it does in language the consumer understands. Put this shampoo on your **HEAD** and there will be no dandruff on your **SHOULDERS**. Die Hard batteries and Close Up toothpaste are two more examples of names that tell you what the product does.

Names are powerful communicators

The Greyhound Corporation had a name problem. When you hear the word "greyhound," what comes to mind? Do you picture a bus headed down the highway with a sleek dog painted on the side? Do you remember television commercials with a bus driver leaning out the window saying, "Leave the driving to us"? Does it surprise you to learn that the Greyhound Corporation was completely out of the bus business for several years before it changed its name?

"Despite all the money spent since the early 1970s," said John W. Teets, chairman, president and chief executive officer of the Greyhound Corporation, "there are still a lot of people who don't know we do something other than drive buses."

Such is the power of a name. The consumer makes a decision about a product, company or service, then places that decision in a box in his mind. Once it's there, it's virtually impossible to dislodge.

Greyhound's solution

The Greyhound Corporation decided to solve its problem by changing its name. First they changed it to "Greyhound Dial Corporation," keeping the picture of a greyhound dog as part of their logo. Management says they made this change because the Dial consumer business is their largest subsidiary. The new name probably did expand the public's perception of the company. Now people thought, "These folks not only drive buses, they also sell soap." Not long after becoming the "Greyhound Dial Corporation" management made another change. This time they went all the way, dropped the greyhound dog and became simply "the Dial Corporation." Much better and now the confusion is gone.

What's a "United Brand"?

The United Brands Company recognized the desirability of having a name compatible with knowledge the business community already possesses. The name "United Brands" didn't tell you what this company did. See if you know what they do when you hear the company's new name: "Chiquita Brands International, Inc."

Of course. This company sells bananas. And since almost half of its product is marketed under the Chiquita name, when you see "Chiquita Brands International, Inc." you know what this company does. The name now fits the positioning strategy.

Domino's considered name change

Tom Monaghan considered changing the name "Domino's Pizza" to one that better reflected what his company did. The name "Domino's" evolved from Monaghan's first pizza store in Ypsilanti, Michigan. That store was called "DomiNick's Pizza." Monaghan's company had grown by acquisition to three stores, all with different names. Monaghan believed in keeping operations as simple as possible so he wanted one name. He couldn't use "DomiNick's" for contractual reasons so he picked "Domino's." "Domino's" had a lot going for it. It was close to the old name, "DomiNick's," so people looking in the phone book could find it. "Domino's" was Italian and it was unique. Monaghan's advertising agency designed the red domino logo with three dots. Each dot represented one of Monaghan's stores.

Monaghan lived to regret his name choice. As Domino's became larger and more visible, the Amstar Corporation sued Domino's Pizza because they said that the name infringed on their Domino Sugar trademark. It took five years for Monaghan to win the suit. He selected an alternate name, "Pizza Dispatch," in case he lost the suit and had to change names. Monaghan opened forty Pizza Dispatch stores while the lawsuit was in process. Consumer research indicated customers actually preferred the Pizza Dispatch name over Domino's Pizza.

So did Monaghan. You can see why. The name "Pizza Dispatch" describes precisely what the company does, dispatch pizza. The name would have been an improvement because it would have focused attention on the company's position, "Home delivery, thirty minutes or less, guaranteed." Changing the name would have been very expensive, however, and there was a lot of history attached to the Domino's name, so Monaghan decided to keep it. Monaghan says in his book, *Pizza Tiger*, that he now feels he should have changed the name.

You name is a key element in your strategy. Be sure that it's a help and not a hindrance.

Be a Tortoise, Not a Hare

Remember the fable of the tortoise and the hare? The hare was a much faster runner but lost the race to the tortoise. He lost the race because he went off on tangents, while the tortoise consistently plodded to the finish line. A consistent strategy focused on establishing and maintaining your position is the most effective use of your resources. It may seem like you're just plodding along, but you'll produce more with less effort and soon own your crackerjack position. So be a tortoise and not a hare.

When the early excitement is over and you've achieved your position, like the hare you'll be tempted to fiddle with what you're doing. You spent a lot of time and effort creating this plan; now you're implementing it and there's no major crisis or stress kicking in your adrenalin. It's hard to resist the temptation to fiddle.

Boredom creates desire to fiddle

As a pilot in the Air Force, I flew the F-86L airplane. The F-86L was a single-engine, single-seat, all-weather interceptor. You've probably seen one up on blocks in front of a VFW hall or in a book picturing classic aircraft.

Since the F-86L was single-seat, you couldn't take a flight with an instructor to learn how this aircraft functioned. You learned in a simulator. A simulator is an electronic machine built to simulate actual flying conditions in a particular type of aircraft. The pilot enters an enclosed room that has the same cockpit layout as the aircraft he's studying. Sitting in the simulator is the same as sitting in the aircraft. Since you can't see outside, all of your flying is done on instruments.

As you became familiar with the simulator, the instructor outside the simulator creates simulated emergencies. She can make the electrical system fail, flame out the aircraft, start fires, etc. As quickly as you solve one problem, she creates another one. By the time you finish your orientation in the simulator, you are used to moving from one crisis to another.

Then you go out to the flight line and climb into the actual aircraft. Once you're in the air and past the early apprehension of flying a new airplane, you suddenly have all this time on your hands. Crises had occurred as fast as you could handle them in the simulator. In the air, no crisis. So you must adjust to routine flying on your way to accomplishing the purpose of the flight. Routine flying has been defined as "hours and hours of boredom separated by moments of stark terror." And you kind of miss those "moments of stark terror" from the simulator. Your adrenalin would like to have a crisis to solve.

So it is with the implementation of your strategy. After experiencing all of the excitement involved with creating the position and designing your strategy, you now settle into the routine of carrying it out. Then there's this temptation to look for more action. You must resist that temptation if you are to achieve your goal.

Tinkering leads to self-tacklization

It's when you start tinkering with your position or dabbling in other activities that you begin to self-destruct. You get fancy and become a victim of "self-tacklization." I was at a college football game when a halfback broke into the clear, headed for a touchdown. No player from either team was within fifteen yards of the ball carrier when, for some inexplicable reason, he cut to his right, tripped over his own feet and fell. The public address announcer said, "Credit Dan Smith with the self-tackle." Tinkering and dabbling leads to self-tacklization.

It's hard to ignore the enticing song of exciting diversions. Remember when you were a kid at Christmas? Visions of new toys danced in your head. All of your present possessions paled in comparison to those expectations. Even when those expectations were never quite fulfilled, you kept having them.

Exploring new paths. Transferring your brilliance and expertise to some new playing field where you can show the current players how it's done. It's all tempting.

Ego can get you into trouble

Diversions like these seem so logical at the time. They seem to be simple extensions of what you're already doing that won't take much time or require much effort. Besides, you might make a little money.

Tom Monaghan hears this same logic from his Domino's Pizza franchisees who want to sell sandwiches, add a few tables or start serving beer. Monaghan refuses to bite.

He refuses to bite because experience taught him the importance of focusing on his crackerjack position.

You think you can do anything

"One of the hazards of success in Domino's," says Monaghan, "is that the grass tends to start looking greener on the other side of the fence.

"You start thinking you can do anything. I was that way back in the early days. I got into frozen pizza for a while and it was a disaster. If I hadn't messed around with those frozen pizzas for the better part of a year, trying to sell them in bars and restaurants, Domino's would be much larger by now. I robbed us of that year's potential by getting off on a tangent."

Once you start one of those diversions it's hard to stop. A lawyer friend once advised me, "There's nothing in this world that is not harder to get out of than it is to get into. Always know when and how you're going to get out if the deal turns sour."

The "Pernell Roberts syndrome"

In show business it's generally called the "McLean Stevenson Syndrome." You may recall that McLean Stevenson starred as Colonel Henry Blake in the hit television series "M*A*S*H." Stevenson chose to leave that role and sank into obscurity as the star of "The McLean Stevenson Show," which quickly failed. That bomb was followed by four other equally short-lived series. Who has heard of him since?

A better name might be the "Pernell Roberts Syndrome." Roberts left a hit television series long before Stevenson left "M*A*S*H." Roberts played the eldest Cartwright son on the television megahit "Bonanza." He chose to leave the show in 1965, eight years before "Bonanza" ended its run. Fourteen years went by before Roberts was able to make it back to prime time television as "Trapper John, M.D."

"Trapper John, M.D." ran for several years. No rumors ever circulated that Roberts was considering leaving "Trapper John." He probably thanked his lucky stars for helping him survive his decision to depart "Bonanza."

Females are not exempt from the Pernell Roberts Syndrome. In 1980, Suzanne Somers demanded a five-hundred-percent salary increase and a ten-percent share of the profits from "Three's Company," the highly successful television series about three unmarried roommates. Four years earlier Somers had emerged from obscurity to star in the program as the sexy, nubile Chrissy Snow. The producers rejected her demands. She left the show, and "Three's Company" continued successfully without her. Somers did not reappear in a network prime time television series until 1991, eleven years after her departure from "Three's Company."

Newhart dances with the one who brung him

Bob Newhart avoided the Pernell Roberts Syndrome. Newhart exemplifies the benefits of "dancing with the one who brung you." Newhart accepts that his comedy is most successful when he reacts to others instead of trying to be the comedic focal point. Jack Benny pioneered this style on radio.

Newhart played a psychologist in his first successful prime time series, "The Bob Newhart Show." His character reacted to neighbors and patients and never cured anybody. The series ran for a profitable six years.

Bob Newhart followed "The Bob Newhart Show" with "Newhart." The name told you that this program wasn't going to be different from its predecessor. The hero in "Newhart" was a writer who bought an inn in Vermont. As a neophyte innkeeper, Newhart continued doing what he does best, react. The inn provided a much broader range of people to react to than the psychologist's office. This show ran on the network for eight years.

Newhart says that when you've found your particular style and talent, you thank God and then you don't change it. He points out that Spencer Tracy and John Wayne were successful because they seldom deviated from their individual styles.

Newhart won't let producers or directors or writers change his style. During the run of "The Bob Newhart Show," the producers wanted to make Newhart's character a new father, opening up all the typical newborn-baby storylines. Newhart said he had only one question, who was going to play his part? End of discussion.

Newhart considers himself fortunate to have discovered what he's good at and to have had the opportunity to play it. He didn't fiddle with it and the result was fourteen years on prime time television. Plans are under way for Newhart's next prime time series. This time the title is even shorter, "Bob." Newhart will play a comic strip artist. Again he will focus on what he does best.

"My character won't have children," Newhart says. "It's hard enough to figure out what makes adults laugh without having to cater to preteens too."

Sunshine Pantry self-destructs

Like celebrities, businesses can self-destruct when they tinker with their positions.

The Sunshine Pantry is an example of what happens when you forget what you've done to achieve a crackerjack position. A delightful little lady owned this small gift shop. The Sunshine Pantry was located next to a major supermarket. The shop did well but not because of walk-in traffic from the supermarket.

One small gift shop is akin to another. The Sunshine Pantry didn't carry anything you couldn't find in one of a score of similar shops. Still, this store was unique.

Sunshine's proprietor knew that she had to be different. So she installed a standard residential cooking range and oven, a coffeepot, and a couple of small tables with chairs. Then she started baking pies.

Baking pies was the unique factor

No other gift store baked pies. Those marvelous homemade pies provided a special reason to visit the Sunshine Pantry. Three different kinds of pies came out of the oven every day. You soon learned that you'd better get to the Sunshine Pantry early or the pies would be gone. You can only bake so many pies in a residential oven. And if a gift caught your eye while you were drinking coffee and eating your pie, so much the better.

Enough gifts caught enough eyes to generate a tidy little income.

By and by our heroine grew tired of baking pies. It was hard work and people fussed at her because she wouldn't sell them a whole pie to take home. She couldn't do that since she had to serve her regular customers. Quitting baking was out of the question because serving homemade pies made her different. The rich aroma of a freshly baked pie sold gifts all by itself. She couldn't stop baking, yet she was tired, so she sold the business.

Pantry quits baking pies

The new owner didn't like baking pies either. And she didn't have the marketing instincts of her predecessor. Financial records told her that Sunshine Pantry profits came from gifts, not pies. Pie sales by themselves barely broke even. She thought her customers came from the supermarket foot traffic so she quit baking. Six months later the Sunshine Pantry was gone.

Strategy must be consistent

A consistent strategy is a critical element in successful crackerjack positioning. Yet company after company, large and small, abandon good, strong, profitable positions to blaze risky new trails. Warner Communications's destruction of Knickerbocker Toys illustrates the folly in that approach.

Consistent strategy builds Knickerbocker

Leo Weiss created Knickerbocker Toys. Leo immigrated to this country in the early 1900s. He arrived penniless but with a talent. Leo was a toy maker.

Leo changed his last name to White and opened a hospital for toys in a New York subway station. You could leave your broken toy with Leo and pick it up a few days later. Your toy would be better than new because Leo was a crackerjack toy maker.

In the 1920s Leo founded the Knickerbocker Toy Company. He dedicated Knickerbocker to building top-quality stuffed toys and animals that would last for generations. Leo didn't believe in toys that went out of style or required spectacular promotion to become successful.

Knickerbocker's reputation grew, and in 1964 Leo was granted the exclusive rights to Raggedy Ann and Raggedy Andy. These dolls were based on books about a lovable rag doll and her brother.

Leo built a new factory in Edison, New Jersey, and Knickerbocker began to grow. Soon other famous names joined Raggedy

Ann, including Big Bird, the Cookie Monster and all the other "Sesame Street" characters. Smoky the Bear, Snoopy, Curious George, Holly Hobby and even the Walt Disney characters became part of the Knickerbocker family.

Knickerbocker shows outstanding growth

Leo had every reason to be proud as he went to the Knickerbocker annual meeting in 1976. He had shepherded Knickerbocker's growth from its humble beginning in a New York subway station to almost $50 million a year in gross sales. Over the previous ten years, Leo saw earnings rise from 12 cents to $3.30 per share.

On the way to that annual meeting, Leo, then eighty-three years old, had a massive heart attack and died. Leo left behind the world's largest manufacturer of stuffed toys and animals. The company's sales catalog ran over ninety pages and featured twenty-two different varieties of stuffed toys and animals.

Warner acquires Knickerbocker

Knickerbocker struggled following Leo's death and was ultimately acquired by Warner Communications, now part of the Time-Warner Corporation. Warner changed Knickerbocker's marketing focus. Warner decided that Knickerbocker's position as the world's largest manufacturer of stuffed toys and animals wasn't enough. So Warner created the Applause division of Knickerbocker and put the stuffed toys and animals into that division to fend for themselves.

Warner changes strategy

Warner then concentrated Knickerbocker's resources on contemporary themes. For example, Knickerbocker manufactured a line of products in support of the movie *Annie*. The movie was a box office flop and so were related toy sales. Knickerbocker moved into plush new offices, added a warehouse and created a line of products based on the Warner Brothers television show, "Dukes of Hazzard."

New offices equal low profits

Whenever a company moves into new offices, you can expect trouble. A friend of mine is an astute investment counselor. He advises his clients to immediately sell their stock in any company that announces a new headquarters building. His reasoning is that company executives will be preoccupied with constructing the headquarters building until it's complete. Consequently, company operations will suffer.

Instead of operations, management will be concerned with such items as how much square footage each officer has, the color of carpet, china selection for the executive dining room and parking place locations.

Warner's strategy destroys Knickerbocker

It's clear that Knickerbocker was already in trouble when the company moved into new offices. Had they not been involved with that project, Knickerbocker executives might not have invested so heavily in products tied to "Dukes of Hazzard." They might have considered the possibility that sales of products associated with a television program will rise and fall with the popularity of that program. The manufacturer has very little control over those sales.

Tom Wopat and John Schneider, the stars of "Dukes of Hazzard," fell victim to the Pernell Roberts Syndrome and left the program over a salary dispute. Audience ratings crashed. Toy sales collapsed. Wopat and Schneider settled with the producers and returned to the program. However the damage was done and the show never regained its earlier lofty ratings. What ratings improvement the program did achieve was too little and too late to save Knickerbocker. In 1982 the Knickerbocker division of Warner

Communications lost $30 million. In 1983, Knickerbocker ceased to exist.

Knickerbocker's executives failed to recognize that their drastic change in marketing strategy was a great risk. When the company quit focusing on time-tested stuffed toys and animals, it became vulnerable to the whims of a fickle television audience.

Successful toys do not have to be fads

"Just because some toys are no longer very popular does not necessarily mean they will no longer sell," said an executive for Toys R Us, the world's largest toy specialty retail chain. "But many stores just try to catch the fads of the times, and when the fad is over they drop it."

Not all toys are fads. Look at Barbie, the fashion doll. Barbie debuted at the American Toy Fair in March 1959. Since then she has become the most popular toy in history. Barbie, her friends, and associated products are now sold in over one hundred countries around the world.

Mattel intoxicated by Barbie's success

Yet Barbie's success almost destroyed Mattel, Inc. Mattel forgot that the market gives you a position when you successfully fill a hole. You don't create the hole, you find it.

Because Barbie was so successful, Mattel believed they could do anything, and they began tinkering. The company almost self-destructed.

What business are you in?

Businesses are encouraged to ask themselves: "What business are you *really* in?" This question is designed to stimulate a business to broaden its thinking and explore expansion possibilities. The classic business school example is the railroad industry. Railroads thought they were in the railroad business when actually they were in the transportation business and should have broadened their activities to include other land, sea and air shipping.

There's no question that it's wise to ask yourself what business you are *really* in, thereby keeping your eye on the continuing developments in your market. The problem comes when a business gets carried away and broadens its thinking beyond reasonable borders. That's what Mattel did.

Mattel gets carried away

In the late 1960s, Mattel apparently answered the question "What business are you *really* in?" with the word "Entertainment." Not a bad answer. Except Mattel interpreted "entertainment" more broadly than was prudent. Management believed it now had a license to pursue anything and everything they wanted in the world of entertainment. Off they went on a treasure hunt.

In 1971 Mattel bought the Ringling Brothers Barnum & Bailey Circus. Mattel paid the Irvin Feld and Roy Hofheinz families $47 million for "The Greatest Show on Earth." The Ringling Brothers Barnum & Bailey Circus is such a specialized business that during World War II the U.S. Government turned to its management for help in developing troop movement systems. It's difficult to see how these skills are compatible with toy manufacturing.

Mattel also added the Ice Follies and Holiday on Ice plus the Circus World theme park.

Mattel didn't forget toys. The company roared into the burgeoning electronic game field, and Mattel's Intellivision electronic games enjoyed early success.

Mattel kept going. Expansions under the banner of "entertainment" included forays into fish tanks, musical organs and movie production. Mattel also bought Western Publishing Company, publishers of children's books.

Mattel unloads circus at a loss

When you gorge at a banquet, you get indigestion. Mattel got more than indigestion. Mattel got sick and almost died.

In March 1982, Mattel sold the Ringling Brothers Barnum & Bailey Circus back to Irvin Feld. They threw in Holiday on Ice and the Ice Follies. Eleven years earlier Mattel had paid $47 million for the circus alone. Irvin Feld bought all three traveling extravaganzas for $22.8 million.

Feld was delighted to repurchase the Ringling Brothers Barnum & Bailey Circus. He had been afraid Mattel might close the 112-year-old Greatest Show on Earth. At the Washington, D.C., party announcing the purchase, Feld said, "The good Lord never intended for a circus to be owned by a big corporation."

Feld understood business he was in

Feld wouldn't take Circus World as part of the package. "We understand the circus," he said. "We don't know anything about running theme parks." Feld understood that you focus on what you do best if you are to succeed. Sound familiar?

Irvin Feld died in 1984. His son, Kenneth, is now the producer of two separate units of the Greatest Show on Earth plus five editions of Walt Disney's World on Ice and the Siegfried and Roy spectacular magic show at the Mirage Hotel in Las Vegas, Nevada. All of these extravaganzas are similar. No theme parks.

Mattel's troubles continue

Explaining the circus sale, a Mattel spokesperson said, "Much of our future is in the electronics business. Nobody here wants to take on the logistical problem of transporting elephants around the country."

Mattel may have thought its future was in electronics, but the halcyon days of home video games had run their course. Mattel's golden success with Intellivision turned to lead. Losses mounted rapidly. In 1984, a week after announcing it was in electronics to stay, Mattel discontinued its lines and sold the remnants to a third party.

To raise cash and stem the hemorrhaging, Mattel bailed out of Western Publishing Company. The company also abandoned fish tanks, musical organs and movie production. In 1984, Mattel sold the Monogram Models division.

Mattel finally hit a winner in 1985 with its Masters of the Universe action toy. Mattel tried to make Masters of the Universe another Barbie. They supported the toy with a massive marketing budget including a Saturday morning cartoon series. Sales rocketed to $400 million in three years. The market then told Mattel that Masters of the Universe was not a Barbie, it was a fad. Sales crashed and Mattel was left with a choked pipeline of unsold toys.

Mattel followed Masters of the Universe with Captain Power. Captain Power was a complex electronic toy designed to respond to signals on a television cartoon sound track. The toy would then interact with figures on the screen. At least it was supposed to do all that. Captain Power had quality problems. The kids lost interest and Mattel was saddled with another $20 million in unsold product.

Mattel's losses continued to climb. In 1985, Hasbro passed Mattel to become the world's largest toy maker.

Barbie is one bright spot

Fortunately for Mattel, during all this diversification activity the company continued to take care of Barbie. And Barbie kept Mattel from totally self-destructing.

Following her birth as a fully grown young woman in 1959, Barbie acquired an entire family tree of friends, relatives and pets. She's lived in at least ten different residences, changed her hair style several times and undergone three distinct facelifts. She's worked in a minimum of four occupations and was a college student. Barbie stays in harmony with the changing world.

"We use every kind of research available," says a Mattel spokesman. "We use attitude research studies, information from the fashion industry . . . but the most important part is testing Barbie with kids. We can have all kinds of charts and graphs, but there's nothing like putting that doll in front of a kid and watching the reaction."

Kids are honest. A friend of mine asked his seven-year-old nephew what he wanted for his birthday. "I don't know what I want," said the nephew, "but I know what I don't want."

"What's that?" asked my friend.

"I don't want any more of those Fisher-Price toys!" he said.

As a result of this market research, my friend no longer gives Fisher-Price educational toys to his nieces and nephews.

From all its research, Mattel programs Barbie's life two years in advance. That policy explains why Barbie was late into the physical fitness boom and appeared in a Western outfit fully a year after the urban cowboy fad had peaked.

Barbie will never be on the leading edge or depart from current trends. You'll never see a Single Parent Barbie or a Gay Ken. Recently Mattel was shocked when a customer opened a doll box and discovered Ken in Barbie's clothes. Mattel investigated and found that a store clerk had made the switch as a prank. Neither Mattel nor the store thought the prank was funny and the clerk was fired.

Barbie is no laughing matter at Mattel. She represents forty percent of the company's gross sales. And Barbie, under the careful management of John Amerman, finally got Mattel back on track.

White knight saves Mattel

Amerman joined Mattel in 1980 after a career selling chewing gum at Warner-Lambert and Ajax cleanser at Colgate-Palmolive. At Colgate-Palmolive, Amerman helped create the popular White Knight commercial.

A "white knight" is exactly what Amerman became for Mattel. While the parent company was losing money faster than Barbie could bring it in, Amerman established a winning track record running the international division of Mattel. He increased international sales fourfold and operated the division profitably.

Amerman did it by focusing on what Mattel does best. He concentrated on its uncomplicated proven performers. Amerman believes in "dancing with the one who brung you."

In 1987 Amerman became head of Mattel, Inc. He applied the same principles that were successful internationally to the domestic operation. He cut staff, closed plants, and focused on Barbie. Mattel continues to add to its Barbie line. Barbie now has Teresa, a Hispanic friend, and Christie and Steven, a black couple.

Barbie's sales have increased forty percent since 1987 to $600 million in 1989. Amerman also gets good mileage from Hot Wheels, the matchbox-size metal cars that are another basic Mattel product.

Focus on what Mattel does well

Amerman's plan is simple: Focus Mattel's operations on established products. In 1987, Mattel began making infant and preschool toys based on the Walt Disney characters. The Disney products have performed well, grossing $135 million in 1989.

Amerman concentrates on the proven performers while cautiously exploring new opportunities. "Caution" is a new word at Mattel. Mattel's previous pattern was to pour money into a new product as soon as it showed any sales potential at all. When the fad was over, Mattel was burdened with unsold toys, unnecessary management levels and excess manufacturing capacity.

Mattel's handling of the Power Glove demonstrates how Amerman has changed that approach. The Power Glove allows kids to control the popular Nintendo line of video games with a wave of the hand rather than a control box. Mattel had over $100 million in orders for the Glove. However it shipped just $40 million worth of product to avoid getting stung by the return of unsold toys. "From now on," says Amerman, "if a product doesn't sell, we'll just cut it out."

Amerman's "dancing with the one who brung you" operating

philosophy works for Mattel. In 1989 Mattel earned $68.7 million on sales of $1.2 billion. Barbie produced $600 million, half of the total.

And in 1990 Mattel paid its first quarterly dividend in seven years.

So a return to basics under the leadership of John Amerman has returned Mattel to profitability. And once again the wisdom of sticking to your knitting, of "dancing with the one who brung you," is verified.

A jet pilot would not be so foolhardy as to create a crisis just to avoid being bored. A business operator shouldn't either. When your strategy is going well, use the time to further strengthen your position. The stronger your position, the less likely anyone will attack it.

Look for Red Cars

When you want to add some excitement to your enterprise, don't look for diversions, look for ways to strengthen your position. Find ways to secure your niche and lock out your competition. If you focus on your positioning strategy, you'll be amazed at how many opportunities will pop up.

It's like looking for red cars. Just driving down the street you're not likely to notice red cars. As soon as you concentrate on looking for red cars, you'll see them everywhere. When you're focused you can take advantage of these opportunities.

Ross Perot founded EDS (Electronic Data Systems) in 1962 with $1,000. Twenty-two years later he sold the company to General Motors for $2.5 billion.

"Life is a cobweb," says Perot. "The lines cross at funny angles. Whether you are successful or not doesn't depend on how good your plans are, especially those five-year strategic plans business schools teach. Success depends on how you react to unexpected opportunities."

Uncle Jim's Mountain Grown Apples

Unexpected opportunities may come from anywhere. When you

are focused you can use your creativity to turn what may appear to be a disaster into a positioning opportunity.

An advertising executive moved to New Mexico and purchased an apple orchard located on the side of a mountain. He began to sell the apples by mail order.

"Uncle Jim's Mountain Grown Apples" they were called, and he shipped them with the following unconditional guarantee:

> "If, for any reason, you find these apples unacceptable, just let me know and I'll return your money with no questions asked."

One year disaster struck. A hail storm marked all his apples. The taste was not affected. If anything the apples were sweeter than ever. But they certainly weren't as pretty.

For some reason Uncle Jim had more orders that year than ever before. He was faced with the alternative of either returning all the orders unfilled or shipping the apples and hoping for the best.

He decided to ship the apples. In each box he placed a card that read:

> "Notice the hail marks on these apples. These are proof of their growth at a high mountain altitude where sudden chills from hail storms help stimulate the natural fruit flavors which give Uncle Jim's apples their incomparable taste."

That year Uncle Jim had fewer money-back requests than ever. His action further strengthened his unique position of marketing mountain-grown apples. He still gets orders asking for "Hail-marked apples, if available. Otherwise, the regular kind."

The Golden Rooster Room

The Nugget Casino in Sparks, Nevada, used specialty restaurants to attract patrons. (See Chapter 13). The restaurant that specialized in chicken was named "The Golden Rooster Room."

Nugget founder Dick Graves promoted each specialty restaurant as dramatically as possible. To attract attention to the Golden Rooster Room, Graves commissioned sculptor-artist Frank Polk to create a model from which a solid gold statue of a rooster could be built.

The Golden Rooster War

At the time, the United States Gold Reserve Act stated that no private individual could have more than fifty ounces of gold in his possession unless it was a work of art. The Golden Rooster was intended to be a work of art, and permission was secured from the San Francisco Mint to construct the statue.

Graves' concept of attracting customers to his casino with the specialty restaurants was highly successful. The Nugget was fun. The food was good, and customers from the Reno-Sparks area, including me, came often.

Graves placed the Nugget's principal attraction, the fifteen-pound solid-gold rooster, on display in a special bullet-and-theft-proof glass case in front of the Golden Rooster Room. Seven months after the Golden Rooster went on exhibition, the U.S. Treasury Department charged that the statue was not a work of art and violated the Gold Reserve Act. Graves pointed out that the U.S. Mint had given him permission to have the rooster, and the Federal Government dropped the matter for two years.

In July 1960 the Treasury Department again appeared and presented the Nugget with an official complaint entitled: "United States of America vs. One Solid-gold Object in the Form of a Rooster." The Treasury insisted the rooster was not a work of art and was therefore in violation of the law, so it would have to be melted down and confiscated.

Capitalize on unexpected opportunities

When you have developed a crackerjack position based on unique specialty restaurants, and when you have an active positioning strategy in place promoting those restaurants, you certainly don't let an opportunity like this one get away. Graves took full advantage.

Soon newspapers all over the country knew about the Golden Rooster and were writing about its battle for survival. After two years of being locked up in a bank vault, the rooster finally had its day in court. At issue was whether or not the Golden Rooster was a work of art or a fifteen-pound lump of gold existing in violation of the law.

The trial was a major Reno-Sparks media event. The courtroom and adjacent halls overflowed with spectators listening to art critics testify that the Golden Rooster was a work of art. A jury of ten men and two women agreed, and the Rooster was freed to return to its special display case in the Nugget near the entrance to the Golden Rooster Room.

It's not often you can invest $50,000 in a work of art and attract hundreds of thousands of dollars in free publicity. It's not often, but when you have a crackerjack position that's unique and therefore newsworthy, and when your strategy is sound, these serendipitous events do seem to occur.

Tinker cautiously

Not only do you take advantage of opportunities to promote your position, you also look for opportunities to modify your operation and stay in harmony with the market. We're operating in a kaleidoscopic marketplace that constantly shifts and changes. If you don't shift and change with it, the marketplace will pass you by. The key factor is to tinker in a way that does not change your basic operation, to be cautious. "Beware of all enterprises that require new clothes," said Henry David Thoreau. It's wise to follow that advice.

Monaghan's mistake with frozen pizza was undertaking a process that "required new clothes." Domino's is in the delivery business with pizza as its product. Advance preparation and distribution of frozen pizza to bars and restaurants is much different from delivering fresh pizza and has its own unique requirements.

Tinker to protect position

Cautious tinkering to protect your position makes sense. The railroads should have tinkered. The railroads knew how to transport goods from point A to point B. Trucks and ships and airplanes are similar to railroads. Trucks transport goods over the roads, ships and barges on the water, airplanes through the sky and railroads on tracks. So railroads moving into trucking, water shipping and air transportation would have been wise tinkering. Such a move would have been a logical extension that protected their original position. The railroads would have capitalized on their strength, the ability to move goods. They would have simply transferred that strength to other methods of transportation.

Contrast that type of tinkering with what Mattel did when it bought the Ringling Brothers Barnum & Bailey Circus. Planes and trains and ships and trucks are similar. Marketing a fashion doll and moving elephants have nothing in common.

Tinkering involves risk

You have to take some risk to keep your position in tune with market changes. If you don't, you may get caught in a rut that will swallow you. That almost happened to the Disney organization.

Disney almost failed

The Walt Disney Company is one of the great business success stories of all time. It's a real-life adventure with fairy tale ingredients, an American dream come true.

Following the death of Sir Walt, the hero of the Disney story, the company fell on bad times. Soon, corporate raider villains hovered over this damsel in distress like buzzards over a corpse, just waiting to have their way with the weakened heroine. Then two valiant knights, Michael Eisner and Frank Wells, galloped on the scene and saved the day. Now all are living happily ever after.

Touchstone Pictures

One of the first tasks facing Michael Eisner and Frank Wells was the rebuilding of Disney's movie studio. They had to breathe life into both Touchstone Pictures and Disney Studios.

Following Walt's death, the Disney management team recognized that today's market had little interest in the traditional G-rated Disney film. They formed Touchstone Pictures as a vehicle to satisfy that demand without compromising the Disney reputation. Touchstone's first production, *Splash*, was successful but controversial. Walt's shadow hung over the company and many longtime employees believed he wouldn't approve of the partial nudity and hints at premarital sex included in *Splash*.

Touchstone takes a different path

The Eisner-Wells team developed a distinct operating philosophy for Touchstone Pictures. Following crackerjack positioning concepts, they looked at what the competition was doing and then did something different. Major Hollywood movie production companies were focusing on big-budget movies featuring major stars. Touchstone chose to produce small-budget movies without big stars that relied on the story to be successful. They went looking for talented people whose careers were adrift and they found a few.

"Our movie philosophy is to go for singles and doubles when we make our films," says Eisner. "If you go for the home run all the time, you strike out a lot."

Strategy works

The new team's first project was *Down and Out in Beverly Hills*, a comedy staring Bette Midler, Richard Dreyfuss and Nick Nolte. The movie was not only a box office hit, it was also very profitable.

Down and Out cost $13 million to make and took in $62 million at U.S. box offices. The movie also grossed more than $10 million in video rentals.

Part of the movie's success came from Touchstone's marketing savvy. As we have seen, giant corporations such as Procter and Gamble and Coca-Cola sometimes believe they can force markets to do their will. P&G learned with Pringles Potato Chips and Coca-Cola with New Coke that it's the market that determines winners, not the company. To be successful, one had better study the market.

And that is what Touchstone did.

Tradition has it that serious movies are released in the winter and comedies in the summer. Touchstone looked at the movies its competitors were releasing and decided to break the rules.

Counter-programming

They released *Down and Out in Beverly Hills*, a comedy, in January. The movie was received as a breath of fresh air among its more serious competitors and finished among the top ten box office hits of 1986.

What Touchstone did is called "counter-programming." You don't try to overwhelm your competition. Instead, you look at what they are doing and you do something else.

Dead Poets Society marketing strategy

Touchstone Pictures successfully counter-programmed again with the release of *Dead Poets Society* in 1989. Summer is considered the best time to release high-concept movies aimed at vacationing students and moviegoers looking for sanctuary from the summer heat. Summer is not considered a good time to introduce a serious movie. Serious movies are launched in the winter. *Dead Poets Society* is a serious movie.

Disney looked at the blockbusters being released in the summer of 1989. Movies like *Indiana Jones and the Last Crusade, Star Trek V* and the megahit, *Batman,* were on the schedule.

Disney saw a hole in the 1989 summer market that *Dead Poets Society* could fill. With all the heavyweight action movies competing with each other, Disney believed many moviegoers would choose a more serious movie. They were right.

Dead Poets Society found a place among the behemoths as a fresh, original movie. *Dead Poets Society* grossed $94.3 million at the box office, good enough for eighth place on 1989's list of top-grossing movies.

Avoid direct confrontation

The success of Touchstone Pictures once again illustrates the wisdom of avoiding a direct confrontation with a well entrenched competitor. If your competitor is making big-budget, major-star pictures, then you look for an opportunity to produce low-budget, no-star movies. If your competitors are releasing serious movies, then you release a comedy, and vice versa. Counter-programming works for Disney and it'll work for you.

Disney created theme parks

Although the movie studio is doing much better, most of the Disney Company revenue still comes from its theme parks. Walt Disney pioneered the development of theme parks and how to run them. Disney's concept was simple: Take an established entity, the amusement park, and add a theme.

"All I want you to think about," Walt Disney told his theme park staff, "is that when people walk through or have access to anything you design or operate, I want them, when they leave, to have smiles on their faces." And the Walt Disney Company works to keep smiles on those faces.

Focus is on "guests"

Every new staffer is trained at Disney University. At D.U., they are taught that a theme park is a show and each staffer is a member of the "cast." The "cast" learns that visitors to Disneyland and Disney World are not customers, they're "guests" and are to be treated accordingly.

Robert Sutton, an assistant professor of organizational behavior at Stanford University, says Disney carefully orchestrates a visit to its theme parks so that people will remember the pleasant and forget the unpleasant.

Un-American not to have a good time

Disneyland is a part of the American culture. You're expected to have a good time when you go there and nobody wants to admit that they don't. Disney does its best to practice image control so that people returning from Disneyland always tell people they had a marvelous time. They remember the rides, the characters, the cleanliness, the friendliness and the opportunity to participate. They forget long lines, high prices and bad food.

Pictures remind us of good times and Disney makes picture taking easy by lending guests cameras without charge. Designated photo sites encourage people to photograph pleasant scenes like the cute shot of Donald Duck or Goofy. These sites do not feature a view of the long line at the ladies room.

Disney tinkers to maintain position

Part of Disney's success comes from the company's willingness to tinker. If you are to keep pace with constant market change, you must tinker. Tinkering means taking a risk. Taking a risk is not always successful. The key, then, is to tinker in such a way that you do not jeopardize your established crackerjack position and to be willing to abandon the experiment when it's clear than it's not going to succeed. Disney also provides a lesson in tinkering.

Disney purchased the Wrather Corporation in order to acquire the Disneyland Hotel and twenty-five prime acres in Anaheim, California, adjacent to Disneyland. Leases of the Queen Mary, the venerable Cunard luxury liner moored in Long Beach, California, since 1967, and the Spruce Goose, Howard Hughes's giant plywood airplane, came with the package.

The Queen Mary

At the time Disney was researching the possibility of constructing a $1 billion theme park in Long Beach. The Queen Mary would be part of this project, so Disney decided to see if it could transfer its theme park expertise to operating the Queen Mary. Disney proceeded awkwardly. One mistake was applying its strict Disneyland grooming code to the ship's employees. The company fired the longtime third officer when he refused to shave the mustache he had worn since World War II. The result was a barrage of bad publicity as the media took up the third officer's case.

Disney recovered and developed a strategy for the Queen Mary. Disney knew no attraction can survive if people visit it once and don't return. People are more likely to return when they participate in the experience. So Disney attempted to change the ship from a dead museum into an energetic live attraction.

Disney adds theme

In 1990 Disney inaugurated a "Voyage to 1939" theme. As each visitor boarded the ship, he received a replica of the front page of the 1939 *New York Times* for that date. Shipboard entertainment featured 1939 musical shows. Ship loudspeakers broadcasted old radio programs.

Disney understands the attraction of live characters so they had "atmosphere talent groups," including Mae West and Clark Gable lookalikes, circulate the decks.

In 1991 Disney featured tours of the ship that explored areas where ghosts were reported to have been seen. Guides made the tour of these locations a haunting experience for guests.

The atmosphere of the period was carefully maintained. Retail establishments such as London-based Harrod's department store maintained ship-board shops, reinforcing the ambiance. There was not a Disney logo or a set of Mickey Mouse ears anywhere in sight, which kept the image consistent. It also kept Disney from being directly associated with the Queen Mary should the experiment fail. And fail it did.

Be willing to abandon unsuccessful tinkering

Disney's negotiations with Long Beach became embroiled in battles with environmentalists and regulatory agencies so the company abandoned its plans for the Long Beach theme park. The company chose instead to build a second California park close to the site of Disneyland. Disney had discovered that the Queen Mary and Spruce Goose held little attraction for children. The company was also unable to attract adults back for repeated visits. In addition, maintaining the ship and its antique appointments proved to be very expensive so Disney canceled its lease.

Still another example of Disney's willingness to abandon unsuccessful tinkering comes from the company's Buena Vista Television unit. Buena Vista had developed a plan to combine with several state lotteries and produce a coast-to-coast syndicated lottery television program. Buena Vista considered the lottery program to be a normal game show. However, market research showed that since people associate Disney with children, they might perceive the program as Disney encouraging children to play lotteries. As soon as that possibility became apparent, Buena Vista canceled plans for the program. Mistakes are not damaging when they're promptly corrected.

Stay in touch with your market

If you're going to tinker successfully, you've got to stay in touch with your market. The Zebco division of Brunswick Corporation knows how to do this. Zebco is the world's largest manufacturer of fishing reels. Zebco recognizes tackle companies are becoming increasingly similar in products and technology. It maintains its leadership position by focusing on customer service. When Zebco looks for red cars it looks for opportunities to strengthen its service position.

Zebco keeps mobile service vans on the road offering instant tackle repair service on river banks, lake shores and in stores. While providing this service, Zebco employees constantly ask customers what they want. Zebco listens, and makes changes. For example, fishermen and fisherwomen have favorite reels. They don't want to be separated from that equipment very long. Ten years ago a customer had to wait three weeks to have a reel repaired. Now Zebco guarantees 48-hour turnaround or they send the customer a free hat.

Employee training

Zebco has an in-house Certified Customer Service Representative training program. The curriculum addresses every area of customer service and consumer values. The course is constantly updated and is currently 73 hours. Surveys asking customers what they expect and how well the company is meeting those expectations determine course changes. When CSRs complete the course they receive a two-grade increase in their job classification and a 10 percent pay raise.

Broaden the market

When you are the market leader your business will increase as the market expands. So look for opportunities to expand your market.

Zebco knows that a boy often learned to fish from his father. They also know there is a dramatic rise in single-parent households. Generally it's the father that's missing from these households.

"That worries us," says Jim Dawson, president of Zebco. "Research shows if a boy isn't fishing by ten, he's a lot less likely to fish as an adult." So Zebco has spent $300 thousand on fishing programs encouraging youths to take up the sport.

America's population is aging. Senior citizens have the time to go fishing and the money to buy tackle. Research tells Zebco that senior citizens stop fishing when they lose their fishing buddies. To solve that problem, Zebco sponsors senior citizen fishing tournaments. Participants make new friends, keep on fishing, and keep on buying Zebco products.

Maintain position by tinkering

The business environment undergoes kaleidoscopic change at a geometric rate. Maintaining a crackerjack position in this chaos requires cautious tinkering. It's important to remember that successful tinkering is done to maintain and secure your position, not to satisfy your ego.

Before Country Was Cool

Crackerjack positioning will work for you as it has worked for me and my clients. I became a believer when I bought a bankrupt radio station in Pueblo, Colorado, in 1963. I experienced what discovering, accepting, developing and capitalizing on a unique position in the market can accomplish. The KPUB story illustrates the crackerjack positioning concepts we have been studying. Today, as markets continue to fragment, these concepts are even more valid than they were 30 years ago.

Questions to be answered

What do you do with a radio station in the poorest six-station market in the country? How can you program a station that only broadcasts during daylight hours so that it will attract an audience large enough to interest advertisers? How can you provide an audience that can only be reached through that station? How do you promote that station? How do you reach potential clients? These were the questions seeking answers.

Surprising answer

My search for answers got off to an unexpected start on my first trip to Pueblo after I purchased the station. I was giving serious thought to playing middle-of-the-road elevator music when I stopped to have lunch. When you're looking for answers you've got to start someplace so I asked my waitress, "What radio station do you listen to?" She answered, "I listen to KPIK."

Surprise! KPIK was a country music radio station in Colorado Springs, forty-two miles from Pueblo. KPIK's signal in Pueblo was marginal and inconsistent. This woman had to be a dedicated country music fan to listen to KPIK.

Different sources, same answers

There were still such things as service stations with attendants who filled gas tanks in 1963. When I stopped at a service station to have my gas tank filled, I asked the attendant, "What radio station do you listen to?"

And he said, "Well, it's kinda hard to hear but I generally listen to KPIK."

At dinner a different waitress in a different restaurant gave me the same answer. An obvious pattern was developing.

Sometimes hard to accept the truth

Country music was not the answer I wanted. I had grown up in metropolitan Oklahoma City. I was a journalism graduate from the University of Oklahoma. I was sophisticated. Country music did not fit that image. This was long before being country was cool.

It was hard to accept what my research was telling me. Still, everything I had was tied up in this radio station. I had to maintain an open mind, move beyond my paradigm, color outside the lines. So I began researching country music.

Country music fit the market

I learned that the simple messages expressed in country music lyrics appeal to blue-collar workers. Where a Tin Pan Alley song might use "rendezvous," country music will say "place." I knew Pueblo was an industrial town with lots of blue-collar workers.

Another authority said that country music attracted ethnic groups. Pueblo had two large ethnic concentrations. One was Hispanic, the other Polish.

Colorado Fuel and Iron, now CF&I, operated a steel mill in Pueblo and was the city's largest employer. CF&I's steel workers were both ethnic and blue-collar.

Keep filling the pouch

Somebody suggested I visit the Silver Saddle, Pueblo's most popular country music night spot. The Saddle was located in a rural area and served only 3.2 beer. Because of a peculiar Colorado liquor law, only places that served 3.2 beer could be open after 8 p.m. on Sundays. I understood the Saddle was jammed on Sundays.

The next Sunday I visited the Saddle. It was so crowded I had to park almost a mile away. I introduced myself to Peggy and Dale Brown, owners of the Silver Saddle. Dale verified the Saddle was always that crowded on Sunday night. "And," Dale said, "you should see the crowds we get when we book a country music recording artist."

Evidence mounts

There was no escaping the message bubbling out of my medicine pouch. The casual comment of a waitress had now become a deafening roar. It was clear that there were a lot of folks in Pueblo who liked country music. It was also clear that the only radio station serving that audience was delivering a marginal signal from Colorado Springs.

Best research may be what you already know

Country music programming wasn't totally new to me. Three years earlier, when I was 27 years old, I had moved to Reno,

Nevada, to manage KOLO radio station. I got the chance to manage a station in a market like Reno at that young age for three reasons. I was a brilliant programmer, a spectacular salesman, and my father owned the station. It helped that KOLO would be the fourth radio station I had worked for and the second one I had managed.

KOLO was in trouble. The station had lost money for some time in spite of frequent management and programming changes.

Cactus Tom made me a believer

I went to Reno several days before I was to become manager to research the market and listen to the station. The first morning I turned on the radio and was surprised to hear country music. It was "The Cactus Tom Show." Tom's voice sounded like he'd spent years hollering at cattle on the range. He ad-libbed all his commercials, and his closing line never varied. From a throat that sounded like it was lined with sandpaper, Tom would growl, "When you go down to see the folks at ABC Western Wear, you be sure an' tell 'em Cactus Tom sent ya."

"Well," I said to myself, "that station is so desperate they'll put anything on the air." I knew my first managerial act would be to get rid of Cactus Tom.

KOLO radio had a sister station, KOLO-TV. Lee Hirshland managed KOLO-TV and had lived in Reno for several years. When I told Lee my plans for "The Cactus Tom Show," he asked me what I knew about Tom. "Nothing," said I. "What do I need to know?"

Lee enlightened me.

I learned Cactus Tom was the most popular media personality in Reno. Cactus Tom was not a weathered cowpoke fresh off the range. He was a former Los Angeles advertising agency executive.

Tom's biggest client in Los Angeles had been a used-car dealer. Tom used country music to promote that account. He discovered that country music fans are very loyal and will strongly support sponsors who provide the music they love.

Tom had burned out on the Los Angeles rat race and moved to Reno. He convinced KOH, the established radio station in Reno, to add a country music program. Cactus Tom became the host.

Cactus Tom's niche

Tom understood crackerjack positioning concepts. He also understood the country and western music audience. He positioned himself as THE country and western personality in Reno. He perfected his unique raspy voice, knowing that when his listeners heard that voice, they would instantly be aware they were listening to Cactus Tom.

Many radio announcers have voices that are misleading. A booming voice may come out of a short, skinny body. Cactus Tom looked like he sounded. He was tall, thin and walked like John Wayne. His face was rugged and weather-beaten. It didn't matter that he'd acquired that robust look driving a convertible in Los Angeles. Weather-beaten is weather-beaten.

Tom drove a white Cadillac convertible. Behind that convertible he towed a sparkling white horse trailer. In that horse trailer was Tom's magnificent palomino. Wearing a big white hat, Tom rode his horse in every parade for miles around. He was often the parade's Grand Marshal.

People loved Cactus Tom. Country music fans loved him because he played their kind of music. Other Nevadans liked him because he symbolized the rich Western heritage of the state. So when Tom asked his listeners to visit the sponsors of his show and tell them, "Cactus Tom sent me," that's exactly what they did.

Tom sold commercials on his program at the station's highest one-minute rate. He added his talent costs on top of that rate and collected his own accounts personally. Tom guaranteed that his sponsors would pay and he wrote a single check to the station. "The Cactus Tom Show" brought KOLO its highest advertising rate with no talent costs and no collection problems.

The only profitable program on KOLO was "The Cactus Tom Show," and it was very profitable. KOLO had been very fortunate to get Tom to join the station when he had a falling out with the KOH management. Hindsight tells me that I should have turned KOLO into a full-time country music radio station with Cactus Tom as the featured personality.

I wasn't that smart. I did not yet fully understand the importance of dancing with the one who brung you. Fortunately I was smart enough to keep Cactus Tom on the air.

The waitress's comment reminded me of the Cactus Tom experience. As we've seen earlier, often the most important research we do is simply remember what we already know.

Developing the positioning strategy

The country music niche was available in Pueblo. That's what them dogs wanted so I decided to go after it. Product differentiation would give the station its niche. Now I had to develop a strategy to secure the position.

New call letters

The name of a radio station is important just as it is with other businesses, services and products. The selection of new call letters was a significant part of the positioning strategy.

The station had been named KTUX. These were excellent call letters. They were easy to remember, and pronounceable. The KTUX call letters had a logical logo association with tuxedos. You could put your disk jockeys in tuxedos for public appearances, etc.

A good name, however, is only one part of what it takes be successful, and the station had gone bankrupt. Now the market accurately perceived KTUX as a rock and roll radio station that had failed, so that meant the station needed new call letters.

I was delighted to discover that the call letters "KPUB" were available. Not only were these letters pronounceable, "PUB" was the government designation for Pueblo. It was surprising that no other station had latched onto KPUB earlier. In many cities the first radio station in the market acquires the aeronautical designation so there is a certain cachet associated with that position in the broadcasting industry. So, with Federal Communications Commission permission, I changed the station call letters to KPUB.

Coping with country music image

Market perception is reality and country music does not carry a high-class professional image. To minimize that perception and impress sophisticated time buyers, everything the station did was top quality.

KPUB used a professionally produced station identification package. The package included musical jingles and introductions to the station's program segments. I believe in specialists so I hired an advertising agency to develop the station's image. The agency designed a superb logo. It was a cowboy hat with the call letters and radio frequency under it and a neckerchief under that. Stationery, cards, and all other printed material reflected KPUB's quality professional image.

Positioning statement

At that time country music and Western music were included in the same classification. Since Pueblo was in Colorado, a state with a strong Western culture, KPUB's positioning statement focused on the Western heritage. Pueblo was the first city of any size when you entered Colorado from New Mexico or Oklahoma. We combined our programming with our geographical location, and our positioning statement said: "KPUB, The Western Voice of the Colorado Crossroads."

Today you seldom hear Western music on the radio. Performers like the Sons of the Pioneers, Gene Autry, Tex Ritter and Roy Rogers are no longer popular. Today's focus is on country music, but in the early 1960s, Western still fit.

Got Pueblo's attention

Strategy in place, it was time to implement it. The station returned to the air as KPUB on March 30. To get our listeners' attention the station played Ray Stevens's recording of "Ahab, the Arab" over and over for two solid days.

Judging from the 150 phone calls we received, "Ahab" achieved its purpose. I was surprised we got any phone calls when you considered the obstacles a listener had to overcome to reach the station.

During the Ahab marathon, the station broadcast the new call letters only on the hour and half-hour to meet the minimum FCC station-identification requirements. So listeners had to tolerate "Ahab, the Arab" for half an hour to get the call letters. Then they had to call information to get the new phone number before they could finally call the station. We were delighted so many people made the effort.

Capturing the country music niche

On April 1, KPUB switched from "Ahab, the Arab" to country and western music programming. We saturated the market with billboards. The posters carried the station logo and the message, "Reach for your dial, pardner." We had captured the country and western music niche in the Pueblo market.

Securing the position

Once the position was captured, everything KPUB did was focused on securing the position from counterattack. We had nothing to fear from Colorado Springs. KPIK had its own market to worry about, and its weak signal couldn't compete in Pueblo. But some other Pueblo station might have decided to go after the same listeners. So KPUB had to secure its position fast.

Resources focused on clear position

KPUB's five-minute newscasts became "The Pony Express Edition of the News." Headlines were "Shotgun News." We had disk jockeys named "Black Bart" and "Dead-eye Dick." KPUB featured a country music hymn every hour. We carried the livestock reports twice a day; as "Sleepy-eyed Don," I had to read them in the morning. I was never sure what they meant, and still can't tell the difference between a barrow and a gilt but nobody ever called me on it so I must have been close.

Involving the listeners

KPUB invited its audience to join the Country Cousin Club. Listeners received membership cards and Country Cousins were eligible for frequent giveaways. Advertisers became "Top Hands" and received wall plaques to identity themselves to KPUB's loyal audience as country music supporters.

We tied in with everything that came to Pueblo associated with country or western. The Colorado State Fair is in Pueblo. KPUB's remote-broadcast trailer was painted like a covered wagon. We took it to the fair and carried live interviews with event contestants and listeners who dropped by the trailer. We enrolled them as new members of the Country Cousin Club.

Staying in touch

Most of Pueblo's leading citizens participated in the 4-H Livestock Auction at the fair. So we did too. I attended and bought prize pigs. I didn't think about it at the time but smart strategy would have been to broadcast the auction. Not only would the 4-H members have received additional recognition but so would the Pueblo civic leaders. I'm still learning.

Looking for red cars

We began working with Dale and Peggy Brown, owners of the Silver Saddle. The Silver Saddle booked country artists on tour. KPUB advertised the shows in exchange for part of the box office receipts and the opportunity to give away a few free tickets to Country Cousin Club members. The KPUB staff went to the shows to meet both the listeners and the artists. Country music artists attracted KPUB's listening audience. The audience provided KPUB a product to sell. It was important to know as much about both the artists and the listeners as possible in order to sell the product to sponsors.

Silver Saddle shows

Most of the shows at the Silver Saddle were handled on a "first money" basis. The Browns furnished the building and made their profit on beer sales. KPUB charged an admission fee and the artist got "first money" from the box office receipts up to an agreed-upon amount. Anything over that amount was the station's compensation for its advertising. If the box office receipts total didn't reach the agreed amount, the artist took all the money and we got the experience.

Country music fans are wonderful people. So are the artists. A warm camaraderie exists between the two. The shows were fun. Educational, too, as I continued to learn positioning strategy from country artists. One star taught me more about positioning strategy than any other.

Buck Owens was different

I shall never forget the first time Buck Owens played the Silver Saddle after KPUB went on the air.

Buck and the Buckeroos arrived early in the day so we could do a live interview on the station. Many artists didn't get to the Saddle until it was almost time for them to start playing. Occasionally one didn't get there at all.

Buck understood his audience

Buck understood that people came to see him and not his band so he was on stage for the entire four-hour evening. Most artists would do two or three fifteen-minute sets during the course of the evening and let the band carry the rest.

Country music fans liked to see their stars in fancy outfits. Buck didn't disappoint them. The Buckeroos' costumes were loaded with sequins and fancy needlework. Buck and the Buckeroos put on a marvelous show.

Buck understood positioning

At the end of the evening Peggy, Buck and I went into the office to settle up. Peggy emptied the box office receipts from the coffee can onto the table and began to count. Peggy was talented. She could count money faster than any bank teller I ever saw. When she was through, there was $518 on the table. Our deal with Buck had been $550 first-money.

Buck took me aside and said, "Don, you didn't make any money on this, did you?"

"No, I didn't," I told him, "but I don't mind. We're working to establish country music in the Pueblo area. You've put on a terrific show here tonight. These folks are going to tell their friends. I don't mind not having made any money."

And Buck said, "Don, I've played the Silver Saddle many times before and tonight's crowd is the best I've had so I know you've been playing my records. I appreciate that, so to help with the expenses of tonight's dance, I want you to have this $50."

I was floored. Nothing like that had ever happened before. Or since.

Of course, if you think we played his records *before* that night, you can imagine how we played them afterward.

Buck built on his strengths

Buck knew what he was doing. He understood crackerjack positioning. He had studied his competition. Buck realized how the typical country artist was perceived. He'd spent years playing guitar in country bands so he knew their work habits. He also understood his market, both his fans and his booking agents. He positioned himself as being different. He promised a lot and delivered more. He gave the audiences what they wanted and worked hard to please those who booked him.

Buck is a talented guitar player who really can't sing at all. He took what talent he had, positioned it through hard work and became a country music superstar as the co-host of the "Hee Haw" television series. Buck now owns a chain of radio stations and has retired from "Hee Haw" so you don't often get the chance to see him perform. If you do get the chance, go see him. You'll see a crackerjack positioning master at work.

Ego leads to self-tacklization

One day, a couple of months after KPUB had been launched, one of my announcers brought this young country singer in to meet me. The singer's name was Bill Goodwin and he was well-known in the Pueblo area.

Bill told me what a great job I was doing with the station. He said that people in his audiences were all talking about KPUB and how much they appreciated it. It was obvious, according to Bill, that I was a fine judge of talent, a brilliant radio station operator, etc., etc., etc.

I could see that Bill was a sensitive man with splendid judgment.

The conversation soon turned to Bill's career. He was confident that he was on the way to the top. He pointed out that his current record, "Shoes of a Fool," was now on the Country Music Top 100 list in *Billboard* magazine. Country music records were not big sellers in 1962, and I later found out that any record selling more than a couple of hundred copies might show up on *Billboard's* list.

All he needed, Bill told me, was somebody with astute business judgment, daring promotional talents and creative vision to guide his career. In short, said Bill, what he needed was me.

It was Christmas Eve all over again. Visions of Colonel Tom Parker guiding Elvis Presley to international fame danced through my head.

Ego ignores facts

The fact that I'd been in country music for less than six months and had never met a live country singer before Bill Goodwin, let alone managed one, never entered my mind. I was hooked.

There was this matter, said Bill, of a little capital needed to pay a few bills. "No problem," said I. "After all, we're soon to be rich and famous." Six months and several dollars later, I realized that when Bill Goodwin sang "Shoes of a Fool," I was the fool wearing those shoes. It wasn't Bill's fault. He believed in himself and what he told me. I was the one who should have known better.

Once was not enough

I wish I could tell you that experience taught me to stick with what I knew best. It took another lesson before I got the message.

One day, two loyal KPUB listeners came to see me. This wasn't long after we had promoted a couple of country music shows at the civic auditorium.

The country music shows had been a wash. They hadn't been

profitable but they hadn't lost money either. Promoting the shows, as long as they didn't lose money, made sense because it was an additional opportunity to strengthen the KPUB position as Pueblo's country music station.

My visitors were budding promoters. They wanted to bring professional wrestling to Pueblo.

They told me that the success of the country music shows at the auditorium proved that I was a "brilliant" promoter. It was clear, they said, that combining their vast knowledge of professional wrestling with my promotional expertise would make us rich and famous. Once again, I was hooked.

Fortunately, we were so inept that our first match never got off the ground. This time my financial losses were limited to organizational costs. I gave up "self-tacklization."

Constantly reinforce position

Fortunately those diversions were not too costly. Those experiences taught me to focus KPUB's efforts on country and western music and the associated culture. If it was country, or western, and if it was in Pueblo, KPUB was involved. KPUB was loyal to its listeners and the listeners were loyal to the station. We could now go to a prospective advertiser and say, "These are the folks who listen to KPUB. If your product fits these people, KPUB is how you can reach them."

Within six months KPUB had the second largest audience in Pueblo. The station became profitable in its first year of resumed operation. Five years later I sold the station for six times my original investment. More important, I had learned first hand that crackerjack positioning concepts work.

I had also learned that they only work if you are fully committed to the task at hand.

Nothing Replaces Commitment

Nothing will take the place of commitment.
Talent will not.
Nothing is more common than unsuccessful
    people with talent.
Genius will not.
Unrewarded genius is almost a proverb.
Education alone will not.
The world is full of educated derelicts.
Persistence and determination alone are
    omnipotent.

Calvin Coolidge

The market provides you an opportunity to establish a cracker-jack position. The market does not give that position to you. You must develop and implement a strategy to occupy the position. And no strategy will work if you are not committed to making it work.

Must give up other options

Commitment means you have to give up other options, all of

them, and focus on establishing your single selected position. The market will not allow an enterprise to occupy two positions at the same time. If you try to do that, you will end up with no position at all. The market will place you in the bone yard labeled "others."

Giving up your other options is the most difficult action you will take. It is the absolutely essential step if you're to establish your crackerjack position. If you do not do that, your crackerjack positioning program will not succeed. *The biggest leap in the positioning process is accepting the crackerjack position you have discovered to the exclusion of all others and then going after it.*

It's a difficult step to take. No matter how many times a person says otherwise, what she really wants to do is to keep all her options open. We hate to make a choice and limit our efforts to that choice. We have a difficult time choosing a single item from a restaurant menu even at McDonald's because we're afraid of what we might miss. You've been behind those people in line. We want it all. But you can't have it all.

Difficult to do

Perhaps this exercise will show you how difficult it is to give up options and focus your resources on one position. You need a piece of paper and a writing instrument.

Fold your paper so that you have four equal parts. Tear the paper into those squares. Pick the four people or things that are the most important to you. Write the name of one person or thing on each piece of paper.

Now pick the person or thing that is the least important of the four that you have selected. Take that piece of paper, wad it up and throw it away. You are left with three pieces of paper, each containing the name of a person or thing. Again, choose the one that is the least important, wad it up, throw it away.

Two papers remain. Choose between the two, wad up the least important paper and throw it away. You have now selected the one person or thing that is most important to you and discarded your other options.

Most people find this to be a difficult task. Yet if you are to succeed in establishing a crackerjack position in a niche market this is the process you must follow. Your resources are simply too limited to try and do it all.

Katharine Hepburn knows you can't have it all

Katharine Hepburn learned at an early age that you can't have it all. During a television interview with Dick Cavett, she said that she had been married briefly after graduating from college. Cavett asked her why she had never remarried.

"Because," said Hepburn, "I realized that you can't have it all. You can't do it all. To take care of somebody is an all-time job. To bring up a bunch of kids is an all-time job.

"I was perfectly willing to do the one thing," Hepburn continued. "Most people won't settle for that. Most people try to lead two or three lives. I don't think you can. At least I can't. Acting takes enough out of me that I can't do anything else."

Singleness of purpose has its rewards

Katharine Hepburn's career illustrates that when you are committed to a single direction and focus all your resources on that commitment, it's amazing what can be accomplished.

My father's record also demonstrates what a talented person can accomplish when possessed by a singleness of purpose. My father was born in Fort Worth, Texas, and grew up in Oklahoma City, Oklahoma. As a youngster, Dad earned money selling newspapers and became fascinated with the newspaper business. He was editor of his high school paper and decided to pursue a journalism education.

My grandfather was a traveling grocery salesman. He didn't see much future in journalism. Down the street from their home was an auto mechanics school. Granddad knew auto mechanics had a future so he tried to convince Dad that's what he should become.

Dad chooses journalism

Dad made his choice. Much as he might have wanted to please his father, Dad committed to journalism.

The University of Missouri accepted Dad as a journalism student. Granddad gave him $50 and sent him on his way. Dad worked his way through college with numerous odd jobs such as shoveling coal into fraternity and sorority house furnaces on cold winter mornings. During the summers, he worked in a slaughterhouse in Oklahoma City because the pay was good.

Dad was hired, and fired, from two newspaper jobs in quick succession following his graduation from Missouri. He went to work in Austin, Texas, determined he wouldn't be fired again.

Commitment to job provides opportunity

Charles Marsh, co-owner of the *Austin American-Statesman* newspaper where Dad was working, noticed he was always there. Dad was selling ads, laying out pages and working on the news desk. When the newspaper owners opened a small photoengraving plant, they offered Dad the opportunity to purchase part ownership and run the plant. He accepted.

Over the next few years, Dad worked with Charlie Marsh in various capacities and locations. Marsh was a trader. He continually bought and sold businesses, generally associated with the newspaper industry. Dad participated in these transactions when he could and saved his money.

Dad's first newspaper

Dad bought his first newspaper in 1936. He purchased the *Evening News* in Quincy, Massachusetts. The newspaper was struggling. Dad turned it around and sold it to his competitor at a substantial profit.

Dad loved the newspaper business. He also was very fond of San Antonio, Texas. So when the opportunity to purchase a brewery in San Antonio came up, Dad took it. My father soon discovered his love for the newspaper industry was greater than his fondness for San Antonio. So he sold the brewery and went looking for a newspaper.

Founding the Donrey Media Group

In 1940 Dad found three newspapers. One newspaper was in Okmulgee, Oklahoma, and two were in Fort Smith, Arkansas. Dad bought all three, and these papers became the cornerstone of the Donrey Media Group.

My father had found his niche. Dad was an expert at running newspapers in relatively small markets. He bought newspapers in these markets, increased sales, cut expenses and made the papers profitable.

Large newspaper groups had little interest in these borderline properties. Dad went looking for them. His typical purchase was a family-owned newspaper. Sometimes heirs could not agree on who should operate the paper. Other times the family simply decided to sell and invest elsewhere. Still another scenario would find the owner ready to sell because his principal heir was not interested in the paper and the owner wanted to avoid a family squabble upon his death.

Whatever the reason, owners of these newspapers found the Donrey Media Group to be the perfect buyer. An owner selling to Donrey knew that his staff would have the opportunity to develop their talents in a growing newspaper company. He also knew that Donrey would invest the capital required to modernize the paper and continue to serve the market. And, because of Donrey's success, the owner knew that he would get his money. So everybody won.

Donrey's strategy

Dad focused on Donrey's crackerjack position as the successful operator of small-market newspapers always interested in additional acquisitions. Donrey actively supported journalism schools, staying in touch with the professors and students as well as other journalism school patrons.

Dad became friends with newspaper owners who fit Donrey's niche. He was delighted to help an associate when he could. For example, a minority owner in a family-owned paper might want to sell his interest. There is not much of a market for a minority interest in a tightly held newspaper. Donrey would often buy the interest. Donrey thereby helped the owner solve an immediate problem and, if the majority interest ever became available, Donrey would be the logical buyer.

Consistency pays off

Fifty years later Donrey continues to follow the same philosophy my father began in 1940. Donrey now owns and operates 53 daily newspapers throughout the country.

Over the years Donrey has invested in other enterprises. These investments were usually in other communications media. The strategy has currently been to solidify and protect Donrey's established position in the newspaper industry.

Donrey began this practice following World War II. The radio broadcasting industry became an important communications medium during the war. People listened to commentators and newscasts to learn what was happening. Some people believed radio would replace newspapers.

Would radio replace newspapers?

It wasn't possible to build new radio stations during the war. The government was not issuing licenses and there was no equipment available. After the war the Federal Communications Commission began to grant licenses.

My father had little serious interest in radio. He's a newspaper man. He's also a realist. Dad didn't believe radio stations were going to replace newspapers. But if they were, he wanted to own the stations.

So Donrey entered the radio broadcasting industry. Dad knew little about radio so in the beginning he went into partnerships with people who did. After learning the business, Dad began building or acquiring stations on his own in markets he understood. These were usually markets where he already owned a newspaper.

Same strategy in television

Dad followed the same strategy in television. As television station licenses were granted, Donrey was in the thick of the battle. Dad didn't think that television was going to replace newspaper publishing any more than radio had, but, again, if it did, he was going to own the television stations.

Dad's primary goal was to protect Donrey's newspaper investments. So Dad applied for television stations in markets where Donrey either owned newspapers or had another outlet close by. Experts often believed these markets were too small to support television stations.

Reno, Nevada, is an example. Donrey doesn't own a newspaper in Reno but it publishes the *Nevada Appeal* in Carson City, the capital of Nevada, located 32 miles south of Reno.

Donrey applied for a television station license in Reno, received the permit and built the station. Experts believed this station wouldn't succeed. The first station manager hung a newspaper clipping on his office wall that reported on a panel discussion sponsored by the Reno Rotary Club. The panel consisted of several advertising experts from the Reno area. These experts explained why Reno would never have its own television station. The market was simply too small.

Reno now has six television stations.

Donrey's strategy, designed to protect its newspaper interests, resulted in its eventually owning four television and seven radio stations.

Return to strengths

There are similarities, but broadcasting and newspaper publishing are different businesses. For example, a daily newspaper seldom has a direct competitor. Broadcast properties always do. Marketing strategy is considerably different when you have a direct competitor than it is when you are a monopoly.

Donrey recognized these differences. Donrey's expertise was running newspapers, not broadcast stations. As its newspaper division continued to expand, the company sold all of its broadcast properties except the Reno television station.

The company's strategy remains the same: Expand and protect the newspaper position. Donrey entered cable television for the same reasons it did radio and television broadcasting. Donrey currently owns five cable television systems in markets where it has newspapers.

My father's persistence, determination and commitment to a single positioning strategy resulted in spectacular achievements. *Fortune* magazine says this son of a door-to-door grocery salesman is one of the 200 wealthiest people in the world. *Forbes* places him in the top 100 of that magazine's annual list of the 400 wealthiest Americans.

Sportsman of the year

Total commitment with a singleness of purpose results in success in other fields as well. In 1978, *Sports Illustrated* magazine named Jack Nicklaus "Sportsman of the Year." In researching the article that would make this announcement, Frank Deford visited Jack Nicklaus's hometown of Columbus, Ohio. In Columbus, Deford interviewed people who knew Nicklaus as a youngster. One was Jack Groat, the golf professional who had given Nicklaus his first golf lesson.

Deford asked Groat if he had known that Nicklaus would become one of the greatest golfers of all time. Groat replied that he wouldn't go that far but he did know that Nicklaus was exceptional.

"Was it because of his exceptional talent?" Deford asked.

"No," replied Groat. "I've had youngsters in my junior golf program as talented as Nicklaus was at that age. Jack was exceptional for a different reason.

"You see," Groat went on, "Jack is the only student I have ever had who, at the age of 10, always came to practice in the rain."

Practicing in the rain

Practicing in the rain. What a perfect expression of what Earl Nightingale meant when he said, "Successful people do what failures will not do, and they make it a way of life."

Nicklaus was asked how he would feel when he could no longer play in the Masters Golf Tournament. He said, "I don't think I'll miss playing in the tournament. I know that I'll miss the three weeks I spend practicing to play in the tournament."

Lombardi calls it "mental toughness"

Commitment, therefore, is the key ingredient. Legendary football coach Vince Lombardi called it "mental toughness."

"I know of no way but to persist," Lombardi said. "Success demands singleness of purpose. Once you have agreed on the price you and your family must pay for success, it enables you to forget that price. It enables you to ignore the minor hurts, the opponent's pressure and the temporary failures."

Commitment is key to success of Federal Express

Frederick W. Smith, founder of Federal Express, knows what Lombardi meant by singleness of purpose. Smith created his concept of an overnight parcel-delivery system and wrote a paper on it for a college economics course. The professor gave him a "C" grade.

The professor may have been right. It was "singleness of purpose" in addition to the concept that built Federal Express. The professor could not have known the depth of Smith's commitment to his idea. He didn't know Smith would become fanatically focused on the idea that the American public would pay top dollar for speed and reliability.

Smith realized that time and reliability were precious commodities. He knew Americans would pay a premium price if they knew that their packages would arrive at the correct destination the next morning.

Federal Express was not an overnight success

It took all of Smith's time, energy and money, as well as all the money he could raise from his family and others, to make it happen. Federal Express was in operation for two years and lost over $27 million before it turned the corner.

Federal Express's voracious appetite for cash brought the company to the edge of bankruptcy on several occasions during its early years. Legend has it that on one occasion Smith had been turned down for a loan so he took what capital he had and flew to Las Vegas. Over the weekend Smith won enough money to make his payroll.

Fred Smith is now considered a genius. He not only built a successful company, Smith founded an entire industry. Several companies now compete with Federal Express for airborne delivery business.

Smith not perfect

Smith may be a genius but he made mistakes. You don't establish crackerjack positions without making mistakes. Commitment makes it possible to weather those mistakes and press on.

Federal Express began by advertising its ability to deliver all types of packages. The marketplace was not impressed. The business did not begin to flourish until Smith focused on the crackerjack position that made the company unique: the "when it absolutely, positively has to be there" overnight service.

Smith also founded Zap Mail, a facsimile transmission system, which he visualized to be an expansion of the Federal Express reputation for timely service. The market didn't agree. Zap Mail lost money and was ultimately discontinued. Now ten years later nearly everybody has a facsimile machine so perhaps Smith was simply ahead of his time.

If you believe, you can weather setbacks

You can't win them all. It takes commitment to weather the storms and stick with your crackerjack positioning strategy.

Jack Nicklaus won the U.S. Open his first year on the professional golf tour, yet he was most unpopular. Nicklaus had soundly defeated the charismatic Arnold Palmer, and "Arnie's Army" of fans would not forgive him. Nicklaus's size and blond hair earned him the nickname "Golden Bear." The crowds used the name in disgust, for they considered Nicklaus to be an overweight young rookie who was lucky and had no respect for his elders. The disdain of the crowds could have discouraged a less motivated golfer.

Nicklaus says that the crowd's dislike did not bother him. "I focused on one thing," he said, "playing golf. The rest took care of itself."

And so it did. Now crowds love and respect the "Golden Bear." Nicklaus has become the greatest golfer in history, with records that may never be approached, let alone surpassed.

Mistakes will happen

My father's newspaper career has not been free of mistakes. One was in Natchez, Mississippi.

Most of Donrey's newspapers are in one-newspaper cities. Dad purchased a competitive newspaper in Natchez, a two-newspaper town. He knew he could increase circulation by producing a better paper, although it would be expensive to do. Dad believed that advertisers would abandon the other, and in his opinion inferior, local paper. He would then be able to acquire it cheaply. The merged newspaper would then operate at a profit.

What Dad did not anticipate was that people in Natchez considered all outsiders, even from the neighboring state of Arkansas, to be "damn Yankees." Donrey ran the better newspaper and did increase circulation. But local businesses continued to place enough advertising in the locally owned newspaper to keep it going. Ultimately it was Dad who sold out, not the competitor.

Purchasing small weekly newspapers wasn't a successful venture for Dad either. It's true that Donrey's expertise was running small newspapers, but some were just too small. Donrey purchased weekly newspapers in Carmel, California, and Eureka Springs, Arkansas, before it learned that lesson. Donrey wound up selling both newspapers.

Commitment means sticking to the strategy

Commitment to a chosen position and a strategy to achieve that position means that you won't run at the first sign of trouble. If you're not committed, you'll revert to your past practices the first time you hit an obstacle. You'll keep on trying to cover too many bases. You'll continue to spread your valuable resources too thin to make an impression anywhere.

Because you are developing a position that is unique, you will get criticism and comments pointing out that you're crazy. Sometimes the comments will come from experts.

Experts can be wrong

In 1926 Thomas Edison was asked about the future of talking pictures. Edison replied:

"Americans require a restful quiet in the moving picture theater and for them talking on the screen destroys the illusion. Devices for projecting the film actor's speech can be perfected but the idea is not practical." Edison himself overcame many rejections. His first teacher called him "addled." Other teachers said that Edison would "never make a success of anything."

Kodak is an expert in photography. Yet that company turned down Chester Carlson's patent on xerography. So did half a dozen other companies, including IBM. Haloid Company bought the patent and formed the Xerox Corporation. Notice Haloid didn't complicate the issue by naming the machine "the Haloid" and then explaining that it made xerography copies.

Never give in

Commitment with a singleness of purpose works when you have faith.

NASA had twenty failures in its first twenty-eight attempts to send rockets into space. Because NASA was committed, man ultimately set foot on the moon.

When Fred Astaire first tried Hollywood he was turned down with the comment ". . . balding, skinny actor who can dance a little." Astaire loved to dance, kept on dancing, and became the living definition of the word "class."

Henry Ford went bankrupt in his first year in the automobile business. His second company failed two years later. Ford's third automobile company is still around and doing rather well.

Dr. Seuss's first children's book was turned down by twenty-three publishers. The twenty-fourth publisher not only accepted the book, it sold six million copies of it.

Sir Winston Churchill was no stranger to rejection and the importance of commitment. After a distinguished early career, he was out of office from 1929 until the beginning of World War II, when he became Prime Minister and led England through the War.

Then in 1945, contrary to almost everyone's expectations, Churchill's party lost the general election. In consolation, the Crown offered Churchill an honor. "How can I take the order of the Bath from His Majesty," he asked, "when the electorate has give me the order of the boot?"

After several years out of the public eye, Sir Winston was asked to make the commencement address at a private school. People were curious what this distinguished orator might have to say to the graduating youth so there was extensive coverage of the event by the media.

Sir Winston was introduced. He slowly made his way to the podium and paused, looking over the vast audience gathered to hear his message. He opened his mouth and in that marvelous oratorical style and tone said:

"Never, never, never, never, never, never, never give in!" Then he sat down.

That's what commitment is all about. And that's what's required to make your crackerjack positioning strategy work.

Motivation Drives Commitment

If you are to establish your crackerjack position, you'll have to make changes. You won't make those changes unless you're committed. Motivation drives commitment. Nothing can be accomplished without motivation. Neither you nor your associates will change your present patterns unless you're motivated, because change is a painful process. You must break old habits to establish new ones, and if you've ever tried to change a habit, you know how difficult that is to do.

Motivation seems complex

Countless studies have attempted to discover what motivates a person to do what he does. People spend years in therapy looking for the answer. Supervisors search for the secret so they can motivate their staffs. Businesses run employee surveys hoping to discover the solution. Speakers build careers delivering motivational talks. People purchase tapes and books in their quests for the answer to the question, "What motivates people? What will motivate me?"

When all is said and done, it appears that we are motivated by two factors, avoiding pain and seeking pleasure.

Motivated to avoid pain

First, let's look at how avoiding pain motivates us. Consider smoking. If you have ever smoked you'll recall that the first cigarette was terrible. It didn't taste good and it made you cough. It wasn't a pleasant experience, yet for some reason you decided to smoke another one and ultimately became addicted. The addiction is what kept you smoking. In spite of what the tobacco company advertisements say, you don't smoke for pleasure, you smoke to avoid the pain of withdrawal.

Started smoking to impress girls

I started smoking when I was in junior high school and discovered girls. Girls were tall and I was short. I wanted to impress the girls that I was special in spite of my size. All the advertisements said that smoking was sophisticated. Being sophisticated would impress the girls. I wanted the pleasure of having the girls be impressed so I started smoking and running around with the tough guys. We wore our hair short on top, long on the sides, covered in grease and combed in the back like a duck's tail.

To be a tough guy I had to carry my cigarettes rolled up in the sleeve of my T-shirt. This was the most difficult part of the ritual because my sleeve wouldn't stay rolled up. It's hard to be tough and sophisticated when you're dribbling cigarettes behind you wherever you go.

Addicted to smoking

By the time I discovered that blowing smoke rings didn't impress anybody, I was an addict. I had started because I wanted to be sophisticated. But I kept smoking to avoid the pain of withdrawal from nicotine.

I was a dedicated addict at that time in my life. By the time I was through shaving in the morning, I had smoked at least two cigarettes. Some days I was well into my third pack when I went to bed at night.

Then the Surgeon General's report was released, which said that smoking was bad for your health, and my motivation began to slowly change. It was several years before the motivation to quit smoking became stronger than the desire to avoid the associated pain.

Seeking pleasure motivated me to stop smoking

When I finally did break the habit, it was not the health issue that motivated me as much as ego. Cancer and heart disease seemed remote. I had been short of breath so I could visualize not being able to breathe because of emphysema.

The fear of emphysema was strong, but what finally got me to quit was a desire for pleasure, the pleasure of feeling good about myself. I had seen people whom I respected quit smoking, and I was impressed, but that was what I expected from them. It wasn't until I saw people whom I didn't respect quit smoking that I stopped, because I felt that if they could do it, then I could do it. It took the fear of not being able to breathe coupled with the desire for the pleasure associated with self-pride to finally make me face the pain I would have to go through to break this addiction.

Change is uncomfortable

Habits and patterns are difficult to change because it's easier to maintain the status quo complete with unpleasant results than face the unknown discomfort associated with change. People, companies, even countries, endure unbelievable conditions in order to avoid the pain associated with change. A person will stay in deplorable working conditions because a familiar environment, no matter how miserable it might be, is a stronger motivational influence than the unknown world that will almost certainly improve his situation. Some people stay in unhealthy personal relationships for the same reason — the fear of change outweighs the pain of the present. You must have a very strong desire to make a change to overcome the comfort of familiarity.

Companies and businesses are composed of people. And, like people, they will continue to operate in self-destructive ways rather than make changes to reposition themselves.

People will self-destruct to avoid change

Consider the merchant whose town has now become a bedroom community for a metropolitan area but who won't change his hours of operation to accommodate his customers because he likes his comfortable pattern. Many people who might shop with him leave early in the morning to work in the city and do not return until late in the evening.

At one time the merchant could have counted on the woman in the family to shop with him while the man was working, but now they're both working in the city. The only time it's possible for them to do business with him is early in the morning or late at night, yet the merchant continues to maintain ten a.m. to six p.m. business hours and curses the big city store that stole his customer. The pain of making a change and giving up his evenings to serve his customer is greater than the pain associated with his ever-declining income.

Avoiding pain is hard way to live

Avoiding pain is strong motivation but we have to twist our life out of shape to accommodate it. That's not a very pleasant way to exist.

We live in a macho society and people are not proud of being motivated by fear of pain. When I ask seminar participants what motivates them, the fear of pain is seldom mentioned. Instead, they talk about the quest for money. Money in and of itself has little value. It would be of no use on a desert island other than as a source of fuel for a fire, and metal money would not even be good for that. Money's use, then, is what it can buy, and physical pleasure is one item that can be purchased. Sigmund Freud believed that the search for physical pleasure was the only motivation, and many examples support his position.

Pleasure seeking comes in many forms

Las Vegas, Nevada, attracts hundreds of thousands of visitors every year who come seeking pleasure. Giant hotels with huge casinos produce elaborate stage shows to provide the pleasure of entertainment. Magnificent buffets satisfy the desire for a full stomach and exotic tastes. And the casinos delight the visitor who finds pleasure in the excitement of risking his money.

The food we eat, the wine we drink, the vacations we take, the sporting events we witness, the movies we see, are all examples of money spent to give us physical pleasure. Ultimately, however, that desire is satiated. And motivation must come from someplace else. You can only eat so much ice cream.

Desire for power

Another motivating force is the pleasure associated with power. Philosopher and educator Mortimer Adler disagreed with Freud and said that desire for power was the strongest motivation. Michael Korda, in his best-selling book *Power! How To Get It, How To Use It*, says, "All life is a game of power." Korda suggests that it's the desire for power that keeps most people working. According to Korda, the use of power will get you a bigger raise, a better job and total control over everyone around you.

Desire for power can corrupt

Certainly the desire for power is a prime motivation in the political world. The democratic system requires that actions be taken by the will of the majority. The power to be able to control that majority is a strong intoxicant. Perhaps no politician in modern day history demonstrates the acquisition and use of political power better than Lyndon Johnson. Johnson provided his peers with services or benefits they desired or needed. In return Johnson demanded, and got, loyalty and support. He became the most powerful president in recent history and was successful in getting significant reform bills passed by the Congress.

However, as John Dalberg said in 1887, "Power tends to corrupt; absolute power corrupts absolutely." Lyndon Johnson believed he had the power to force his conclusions on the American people. He decided not to tell them what was really happening in Vietnam, and that decision led to his downfall.

Power important in corporate world

The desire for power is also an important motivation in the corporate world. The power to control the destinies of companies as well as other human beings carries with it an aura that people recognize. When I give a talk to an organization, I notice in some companies that people are hesitant to laugh until they see how a story is being received by their supervisor. They don't want to run afoul of his power.

Corporate power trappings include private parking places, keys to the executive washroom, corner offices, access to company jets, and generous expense accounts. These are strong incentives, for they establish the pecking order and signify who's important and who isn't. Even seemingly minor matters like Christmas card lists are significant. Few things have impressed me as much during my corporate career as the efficiency with which Christmas card lists are maintained. Corporate affairs would run much more smoothly if all actions were handled as well.

When I joined my father's company, the Donrey Media Group, as a vice president, I was amazed at how fast I was added to a substantial number of Christmas card lists. Not only did I receive an avalanche of Christmas cards, I also got presents from suppliers. When I left Donrey some years later, I vanished from those lists just as fast. The cards and presents did not go to a person, they went to a position of power.

Praise and recognition as motivating force

Still another motivational force is praise and recognition. Napoleon recognized the motivating power of praise and recognition when he said, "Give me ribbons and I will give you an army."

Mary Kay Ash built her company, Mary Kay Cosmetics, on praise and recognition. The company stages periodic seminars in Dallas, Texas, at the Convention Center that are described as "a combination of the Academy Awards, the Miss America Pageant and a Broadway opening!" Educational classes are held, but the feature events are award nights when outstanding Mary Kay salespeople parade across the stage in bright red jackets and tell their personal success stories. Mary Kay presents pink Buicks and Cadillacs to the top producers. The premiere event is the night that the Director and Consultant Queens are named in each category. They receive diamonds and minks and are surrounded by a court of women who have also achieved extraordinary sales records.

Praise and recognition are heady motivational stimulants, but like other motivational methods based on external rewards, they ultimately lose their power.

Love what you're doing

The strongest motivational forces are internal. One such force is a love for what you're doing. It's easier to love what you're doing when it springs from your strength, which is why building on strength is such an important factor in crackerjack positioning.

Nicklaus loves playing golf

Jack Nicklaus goes to a golf course well in advance of a tournament. He plays the course over and over again, measuring distances and visualizing shots. Nicklaus was asked how he was able to develop the discipline required to put in so many hours of practice.

"Simple," he said. "I love to play golf."

Dad loves newspaper business

I asked my father what had motivated him to work his way through college and become focused on the newspaper business. First he said it was money. Then he smiled and said, "After the first $100,000, the money didn't really matter. It was simply how you kept score. I kept at it because I love the newspaper business."

Bill Russell loved playing basketball

Bill Russell, the legendary Boston Celtic basketball player, said that he played basketball, not for money or honors, but for those rare periods when it all came together. Both teams would be playing at their peaks and would levitate to a new level. The competition would be white hot, yet Russell didn't feel competitive. It was magic time and these moments sent chills pulsing up and down Russell's spine. The practices, the travel, and the travail were the price he paid for these moments. And the price was worth it to Russell because he simply loved to play basketball.

James Fixx loved to run and hit it big

James Fixx wrote *The Complete Book of Running*, and it became a runaway best seller, vastly surpassing everybody's expectations. Fixx had spent the previous ten years in magazine editorial positions, writing very little. He said, "I was bored and restless. The work I was doing wasn't what I wanted to do, and I therefore did not do it very well."

A fortuitous series of events made it possible for Fixx to return to writing on a full-time basis. *The Compete Book of Running* was the result.

In *Jackpot*, a book Fixx wrote about *The Complete Book of Running* experience, he quotes Larry Batson, a columnist for the *Minneapolis Tribune*, who said "Fixx . . . is in something like the delightful predicament, described by Charles Lamb, of doing good by stealth and being discovered by accident. Fixx wrote a book on running simply because he loves it. It turned out that tens of thousands of people were waiting for just such a book."

When Fixx built on his strength, his ability to write, and then used that strength to write about a sport he loved — running — he created a best seller. It was his love for what he was doing that made it possible.

Jim Henson loved the Muppets

Jim Henson loved his Muppets. He tried for twenty years to get the television networks to give his unique puppets a program of their own. The Muppets had been successful on local television in Washington, D.C., and as guests on numerous network programs. Rowlf the Dog was a popular fixture on "The Jimmy Dean Show" and the Muppets were regulars on public television's "Sesame Street," but the commercial networks refused to budge. Henson and his wife believed in their characters and their ability to entertain, so they did not give up. Finally Sir Lew Grade, an aggressive English impresario, agreed to produce "The Muppet Show" in syndication. "The Muppet Show" became so successful it was carried by more stations in the United States than any major network could have delivered. The show was aired in over one hundred countries and became enormously popular.

"After that," said Bernie Brillstein, Henson's agent, "Jim kind of belonged to the world."

Henson's Muppets became a multi-million-dollar enterprise. Henson created new characters and made feature movies. In the spring of 1990, not long before his death from pneumonia at age fifty-three, Henson was negotiating the sale of his business to the Walt Disney Co. for over $150 million. Henson's love of his work and his commitment to the Muppets made it happen. At his funeral, Henson's daughter Cheryl recited his words, which explained his motivation. "I believe in taking a positive attitude toward the world. My hope is to leave the world a little bit better than when I got here."

Strongest motivation is a sense of purpose

Sometimes you love what you are doing because it's what you do well; other times you love what you're doing because you can see a purpose beyond the immediate effort you're making. You can see that what you're doing gives a meaning to your life.

Viktor Frankl in his book, *Man's Search for Meaning*, says, "Man's main concern is not to gain pleasure or to avoid pain, but rather to see a meaning in his life." Frankl's book describes his experiences in surviving the holocaust as a prisoner at Auschwitz during World War II. It was there that he learned that "a man who becomes conscious of the responsibility he bears toward a human being who affectionately waits for him or to an unfinished work will never be able to throw away his life. He knows the 'why' of his existence and will be able to bear almost any 'how.' "

Such a man has a sense of purpose. A sense of purpose is seldom handed to you. You decide to have it. It comes from within and only you can discover it. To discover it, you must be true to yourself.

David Murphy

Mike Royko, the *Chicago Tribune* columnist, tells the story of David Murphy, a Chicago attorney. It seems that Murphy received a call one day from an elderly lady in Los Angeles. She had a real estate problem in Chicago and had been referred to Murphy by one of his law school friends.

Murphy specializes in management and labor law but took care of the problem. He believed that she didn't have any money so he didn't send her a bill. Murphy handled a couple of other matters for her, each time not sending a bill.

One day he received another call. The woman had returned to Chicago, was in the hospital, and wanted Murphy to write her will. Much to his surprise, Murphy learned that she had $25,000 in cash and a certificate of deposit for $110,000.

The woman wanted to leave modest bequests to nieces and

nephews who had occasionally been nice to her. She planned to leave the balance of her estate to Murphy because of what he had done for her. Murphy refused to write the will. She was insistent so he found her another attorney. She subsequently died, leaving most of her $140,000 estate to David Murphy. Murphy had just placed his mother, who had Alzheimer's disease, in a nursing home and the money would have helped pay those expenses. Or the money could have bought a membership in a private club, or perhaps a new car. Nonetheless, Murphy refused to accept it and had the estate distributed to the nieces and nephews.

When Royko asked him why he turned down the bequest, since it was clearly the woman's wishes, Murphy replied, "Lawyers, rightly in many instances, are thought of as crooks and sharks. Most lawyers aren't, but if I'd followed through on this, I would have added to that reputation. You know, the law and the real world aren't necessarily the same. So a good lawyer has to have ethical canons. It's not just a matter of what is legal."

David Murphy operates out of a sense of purpose that is in the best interest of the profession that he loves. It occasionally requires him to make personal sacrifices, but in the long run it inspires him to be the crackerjack he was intended to be.

Purpose goes beyond personal interests

Purpose, then, is a service to others that is beyond your own personal interests. It may be beyond your immediate personal interests, but it is definitely in the long-term best interests of your business. It's been said that the primary purpose of a business is to make a profit. Yet a company focused on making a profit to the exclusion of all else will not survive. Can you imagine a salesperson calling on you and saying, "The purpose of my call today is to make a profit for my company and a little commission for myself. Now, how can I help you?" You would promptly escort the salesperson to the door.

It takes more than a sense of purpose

If it's to be successful, a business must first operate out of a sense of purpose to serve others and then make a profit in the process. Without a profit, there will not be a return on the invested capital, or rainy day money, or funds for development and expansion. Again, the business will ultimately fail.

Occasionally when I was managing shopping centers, prospective tenants would talk with me about renting space for businesses. When I asked what their positions were going to be and why consumers would buy from them rather than their competitors, they would tell me that their goal was to serve mankind and that the Lord would provide.

These people were sincere, and their hearts were in the right place. However, as pleasantly as possible, I would point out that the Lord helped those who helped themselves. I would remind them that the free enterprise system takes no prisoners, and without a position in the marketplace, it's highly unlikely the Lord will send customers to spend money with them. Simply doing good is not enough. They didn't want to hear those comments, so they would go away to find somebody more enlightened.

Walter Kruse's approach

Contrast that with Walter Kruse's approach. In 1981, Walter came to me with a plan. Walter had been a retailer for sixteen years. Most recently he had managed the children's clothing division of a regional department store chain that was in the process of merging itself out of business. Kruse was aware of the baby boomlet under way as the original baby boomers reproduced themselves. His plan was to open a specialty children's store in our largest shopping center. The name of his store was "Teddy's for Kids." The logo was a teddy bear.

Walter did his research

Walter wanted the location directly across the parking lot from the

C.R. Anthony Department Store because he knew that C.R. Anthony's had the highest gross sales of the dozen Anthony stores in metropolitan Tulsa. High gross sales meant high customer traffic, and Walter wanted a shot at that traffic. He understood the C.R. Anthony's customer because it was the same person who shopped at the department store organization he had just left. He knew that the Anthony customer looked for value but also wanted a wider selection of children's clothes. And they wanted service.

Walter knew his customer
"They'll come to a specialty store because they want the attention a specialty store can give," Walter said.

"Especially in children's wear," he went on. "People have a great many questions about the items they buy. New parents, grandparents or friends buying gifts are not sure of themselves. They need the help they can get from a specialty store that understands their needs."

Walter understood crackerjack positioning
Walter's strength was retailing, so he built on it. He understood the market trends, so he got in line with them. He understood the limitations of his competitors and he understood his potential customer, so he created a position to capitalize on both. Walter developed a strategic plan and put that plan into action. He chose a name that described what he did. He targeted his market with his location. He advertised the advantages of dealing with a specialty children's store and oriented promotions like his annual Easter egg hunt toward his market. Walter had fun and he made money.

Crackerjack positioning program is successful
In five years, "Teddy's for Kids" grew to a five-store chain from its start in our center. Gross sales at the original location increased 300 percent over that period. "Teddy's for Kids" was built on the

service to its customers that only a specialized retail establishment can provide, and it was successful during a period when the Small Business Administration reported children's stores to have the highest failure rate in retailing.

"Those failures suffered from the 'cute' factor," said Walter. "These are often mom and pop stores that know nothing about the business but have a romantic idea that it would be fun to sell tiny baby clothes. We weren't a mom and pop operation in our attitude from the beginning. We tried to use some of the same techniques and methods a large department store would use insofar as determining what the customer wanted and how to present it."

"Teddy's for Kids" was firmly established in northeast Oklahoma when Walter's partner decided to retire. Walter considered the situation. He was astute enough to recognize that the baby boomlet had passed. And whereas the Oklahoma economy was stabilizing following the oil bust, it was unlikely to grow a great deal in the near future. So Walter concluded that his partner had a pretty good idea and they liquidated the business.

But Walter didn't retire. Instead, he continues to serve with a sense of purpose. Walter is currently the Small Business Coordinator for the Central Oklahoma Vocational Technical School. He teaches and consults with small businesses, giving them the benefits of his experience.

You may already have a sense of purpose

You may think that a sense of purpose built on service to others doesn't fit your enterprise. The truth is, you may already be practicing it and not realize it.

The following exercise will help you discover if that's the case. The exercise involves looking at your attitude and your behavior under different circumstances. For the purposes of this exercise, "Attitude" is what is going on in your mind or what you're feeling, and "Behavior" is action that you take.

Across the top of a sheet of paper, write, "When I am at my

BEST" and under that write "Attitude." Then list what is going on in your mind, what you're feeling, when you're performing at your best. "Performing at your best" means everything is falling into place, all is going well and you feel good about what you're doing. Write quickly and put down whatever comes to mind. Your list might have comments like "confident" or "happy." You get the idea, so make your list now.

After you've exhausted your "Attitude" list, write "Behavior" and list what you *do* when you're at your best. This list might include activities like "smile" or "prepare."

When you've finished the two "At my BEST" lists, repeat the exercise to discover what you think and do "When I am at my WORST." Here you might list thoughts or feelings like "discouraged" and behavior such as "looking for another job."

Now review the lists. Ask yourself this question: "When I am at my BEST, where am I focused?" And the answer might be: "When I am at my BEST, I'm focused outward . . . on the needs of others." It follows, therefore, that "When I am at my WORST, I'm too focused inward . . . on myself."

So you see, when you're thinking and performing at your best, you may already be operating out of a sense of purpose, a service to others. When you're at your worst, you may be too focused on yourself. The good news is that your thoughts and performance are controlled by where you are focused. And you can determine what your focus is. The task then is to see how this sense-of-purpose operating philosophy can be adopted as the motivational force in implementing your crackerjack positioning strategy.

No commitment without motivation

We now see that commitment is driven by motivation. Avoiding pain will motivate us but the price is high. External rewards are also motivational stimulants but ultimately lose their power. Motivation that will sustain our commitment over the long run will have to be internal. It can come from a love for what we are doing or from a sense of purpose. Everybody wins when your crackerjack position is maintained through a commitment to a strategy founded on a combination of a love for what you are doing and a sense of purpose.

Listen to Carolyn Miley

So there you have it. Crackerjack positioning will give you the opportunity to succeed in today's market environment. The process is simple. You analyze your capabilities to see what makes you a crackerjack. You check the market climate, including a close look at your competition, until you find the opportunity to capitalize on your capabilities. When you find the market niche, you create a position built on your capabilities to fill it. Next, you develop a strategy to establish and secure the position. Then you implement the strategy. Finally you tinker with your position to stay in harmony with the constantly changing market. The result is a crackerjack position that allows you to produce more with less effort and have a good time in the process.

Commitment is the secret. Without commitment, nothing happens.

When I was in junior high school, my mother asked a friend of hers, Carolyn Miley, to tutor me in Latin. As Mrs. Miley and I became friends, she inspired me to enter a speaking contest. I didn't win, I didn't even place; but I enjoyed it, and that experience planted the seed that grew into my later interest in speaking.

Carolyn Miley was a magnificent lady, and one of my most prized possessions is a portrait of her painted by my mother. My mother studied art at the Chicago Art Institute and later specialized in portrait painting.

I was going through my mother's papers following her death and found a fragile letter brown with age. It was from Carolyn Miley written many years earlier.

Darling:

This note is supposed to PUSH. Technique develops peculiarly. Sometimes we seem to be standing still no matter how much we practice. Yet, if we would go on, we must keep practicing every day at a regular time. That practice should never be *intermittent*, but steady and regular. We feel we are getting nowhere because we do not seem to be improving. Then one day an increased skill is right out of the blue just there. As if by a miracle it bursts forth like a green shoot from a seed.

It is true in golf, it's true in music. I'm sure it's true in painting. That is the way it always comes.

When I was fooling with golf once, the pro told me I was as good as ninety percent of the women who played on the course and that I'd be no better than I was for a year, but that if I played *every* day for that year, I'd step up with that other ten percent who could really play.

In music it is the same. We get so far and no farther, we get disgusted but we keep on, practicing exercises and "pieces" slow and fast, carefully and with abandon — no better — then one day it just bursts forth with ease, a skill has been developed. We have reached a new plateau.

So I say to you: Practice and practice from photographs, from anyone who will sit. Don't wait for the mood but every day, every day, every day, even when it is drudgery and the mind pulls back and back. Don't get annoyed because your vision exceeds your skill, pull up your skill.

"A man's reach should exceed his grasp or what's a heaven for?"

When I urge you, I urge myself — let's go.

Then welcome each rebuff, that turns earth's smoothness rough, that bids nor sit nor stand but GO!"

Do you want to be like all these other dabblers? I wonder!

> Lovingly and pushingly,
> Carolyn Miley

Is there any better way to live?

Suggested Further Reading:

Bolles, Richard. *What Color Is Your Parachute?* Berkeley, CA: Ten Speed Press, updated yearly.

Fields, Debbie, and Alan Furst. *One Smart Cookie.* New York: Simon & Schuster, 1987.

Frankl, Viktor E. *Man's Search For Meaning.* Boston: Beacon Press, 1959.

Hawken, Paul. *Growing A Business.* New York: Simon & Schuster, 1987.

Hoff, Benjamin. *The Tao Of Pooh.* New York: E.P. Dutton, 1982.

Kami, Michael J. *Trigger Points.* New York: McGraw-Hill, 1988.

Kornfeld, Lewis. *To Catch A Mouse, Make A Noise Like A Cheese.* Englewood Cliffs, N.J.: Prentice Hall, 1983

LeBoeuf, Michael. *How To Win Customers And Keep Them For Life.* New York: G.P. Putnam, 1988.

Levinson, Jay Conrad. *Guerrilla Marketing,* Boston: Houghton- Mifflin, 1984.

Levinson, Jay Conrad. *Guerrilla Marketing Attack.* Boston: Houghton-Mifflin, 1989.

Lynch, Peter, with John Rothchild. *One Up On Wall Street.* New York: Simon & Schuster, 1989.

Marcus, Stanley. *Minding The Store.* Boston: Little, Brown and Company, 1974.

Marcus, Stanley. *Quest For The Best.* New York: Viking Press, 1979.

McKenna, Regis. *The Regis Touch.* Reading, MA: Addison-Wesley, 1985.

Monaghan, Tom, with Robert Anderson. *Pizza Tiger.* New York: Random House, 1986.

Naisbitt, John. *Megatrends.* New York: Warner Books, 1982.

Oliver, Thomas. *The Real Coke, The Real Story,* New York: Random House, 1986.

Peters, Tom, and Nancy Austin. *Thriving On Chaos.* New York: Alfred A. Knopf, 1987.

Phillips, Michael, and Salli Rasberry. *Marketing Without Advertising*. Berkeley, CA: Nolo Press, 1986.

Ray, Michael, and Rochelle Myers. *Creativity In Business*. Garden City, N.Y.: Doubleday, 1986.

Reeves, Rosser. *Reality In Advertising*. New York: Alfred A. Knopf, 1973.

Ries, Al, and Jack Trout. *Positioning: The Battle for Your Mind*. New York: McGraw-Hill, 1980.

Ries, Al, and Jack Trout. *Marketing Warfare*. New York: McGraw-Hill, 1986.

Ries, Al, and Jack Trout. *Bottom-Up Marketing*. New York: McGraw-Hill, 1989.

Tzu, Sun, forward by James Clavell. *The Art Of War*. New York: Delacorte Press, 1983.

von Oech, Roger. *A Kick In The Seat Of The Pants*. New York: Harper & Row, 1986.

Index

Order Form

CRACKERJACK POSITIONING

If your local bookstore is out you may order additional copies of *CRACKERJACK POSITIONING*, Niche Marketing Strategy For The Entrepreneur, by sending a check for $21.95 (please add the following for postage and handling: $3.00 for the first copy, $1.50 for each additional copy) to:

> Atwood Publishing
> 5301 S. S. Sheridan, Suite 524
> Tulsa, Oklahoma 74145

Don Reynolds Jr. is available for consulting and speaking engagements. You may contact him at:

> 8086 S. Yale, Suite 252
> Tulsa, Oklahoma 74136-9060
> Phone: (918) 459-0110
> FAX: (918) 459-0110
> 1-800-662-4732